# STORIES
# CENTER STAGE
## Storytelling in Modern Oklahoma-
### *A Brief Survey*

Marilyn A. Hudson

Subject: Storytelling – Oklahoma – 20th Century.

American Storytelling – Oklahoma – History – 20th Century.

027.6251  /  GR  72.3  H88
Published by Whorl Books
Designed by Whorl Books

## Acknowledgement

Thanks to the artists who provided images and bio information for this work. A special thank you to Chester Weems for use of his photographs in this work. Chester has photographed numerous events and performers over the years.

# DEDICATION

To all the story artists who have delighted audiences large and small by sharing stories. To all those, through the power of story, caught our imaginations in cozy rooms, libraries, vast public halls and crowded classrooms. From the uncertain and nervous novice braving their first performance to the experienced teller who mastered their place on stage with high skill years ago, this work is dedicated. To all those who, through their advocacy, financial support, creative vision and appreciative listening, have made storytelling survive to be enjoyed by new generations, our deepest thanks and appreciation.

Marilyn A. Hudson

*The audience enters the auditorium, they settle into their seats with low murmurs, a cough or two, all muted by the heavy curtain of the stage.*

*In the wings, they pause, these people of story, they are a little nervous, a little preoccupied, and even anxious for the moment when the drapes pull back to reveal the empty stage.*

*The house lights dim, a rustle as the curtains open...the echo of footsteps heading to the spotlight and the center of the stage...*

# CONTENTS

# ACKNOWLEDGMENTS

The reasons for this work were simple in the beginning. Showcase the art of storytelling in modern Oklahoma, chronicle some of the events and people involved, and provide for the reader some new information about the art form. To do that, however, required some help.

A big thank you to all those people who shared memories, biographies, resources, files because without that assistance valuable information might have been lost. Listing people always presents the possibility of overlooking someone. I will say simply that represented here is the common memory of the story tellers and the story listeners. There were some who wished to remain nameless but shared their memories and impressions and that is deeply appreciated.

Invitations to submit names, biographies and stories related to Oklahoma's history of storytelling began in the fall of 2012. Individuals in several state and regional storytelling organizations, state library systems and many public groups were invited to share their information and memories. The names listed are not comprehensive and should be expanded to include more information and significant events. Thank you, however, to those who shared names and events they thought were important.

Storytelling is a symbiotic relationship: for every story teller there has to be a story listener. Thanks to all those listened, praised, remembered and shared what they had learned because they complete the circle of a story.

# INTRODUCTION

Like an artist outlining the detailed work of a major painting, this brief history seeks merely to survey and to introduce the history of the oral storytelling art form in modern Oklahoma. Oral storytelling in this work refers to the *art of sharing stories or anecdotes through speech (oral communication) for purposes of entertainment or education.*

This work focuses on the experiences of storytelling in schools, churches, libraries, and community venues. It does not attempt to provide a detailed history to every event, person, or group supporting the art. It does hope to provide a starting place for future research into oral art forms and folk ways in the state. It hopes to initiate a dialogue of the art in Oklahoma that acknowledges its past, recognizes its present and plans for a stimulating future.

Unfortunately, many of the innovators and mentors of the art are no longer living. The memory of these pioneers live on in hearts touched through their stories, the support they provided, or the people they inspired and taught.

Many mentors through the years were never formal performers. They used the art in the process of teaching or in their library work. Many others were family members, neighbors, local farmers, shopkeepers, oil field workers, farm workers, miners, rail crews, ministers, business people, cowboys, bandits and bankers.

As in ancient days, the rivers of storytelling creativity emerged from a blending and fusion of the many small, unique creative streams flowing out of Native American, Scots-Irish, African-American, Polish, German, Asian, and other European cultures. Stories, like other artistic pursuits through time, were always strengthened through interaction, adaptation, and sharing. As a result, strands of story traditions fall across the state from every community, occupation, culture, and region. Like colorful ribbons rippling in a prairie wind they simply wait to be woven into a unique Oklahoma storytelling fabric.

Many outstanding works have addressed the sociological, anthropological, and linguistic influences of art in the state. In works such as B.A. Botkins' *Folks Say* and the WPA Interviews (and other sources), many important oral traditions and folkways were identified and preserved.[1]

Another limitation of this work is its decision to restrict recounting in-depth experiences among ethnic populations, especially Native American groups.  There are so many excellent popular and academic works already available addressing this crucial topic. Such works have previously provided exceptional scholarship chronicling the important storytelling, linguistic, and folkloric history of several ethnic and cultural groups populating state history.  In this work there was a goal of a readable, easily understand primer of the art as it was experienced among most community dwellers.

It is hoped that this simple work might inspire others to dig deeper and across a wider field. There is much work still to be done in adequately identifying, recording, and interpreting the storytelling experience and history within many of these groups. This makeup of those who settled the twin territories (and later the state of Oklahoma) were incredibly

---

[1] B.A. Botkins, Folks Say: A Regional Miscellany (University of Oklahoma, 1930)   ; T. Lindsay Baker and Julie P. Baker. WPA  Oklahoma Slave Narratives  (University of Oklahoma, 1996)  : See in particular, Dayna Bowker Lee's "Folklife in Oklahoma: Sharing the Wealth of our Tradition" and  Roger Harris' "It Was In This Way": The Influence of Oral Tradition on Life and Literature  of Oklahomans." ; "Oral Tradition, American Indian" and "Te Ata (1896-1995)", Encyclopedia of Oklahoma (online)

diverse.

Still to be studied are also the story art experience within *contemporary* Oklahoma's Native American, African American, Asian and European groups, including Hispanic groups. Their stories are tremendously important to state and national history and are worthy of more in-depth attention. There is need of study of how the art form is being maintained, transmitted, and transformed in modern society.

Oklahoma stands singular among the states because of its unique history. For the city and rural dwellers of the nation, it was first a land forgotten because it was in the wilderness. Later it had a controversial identity as a centralized home for relocated Native Americans. Still later, it was viewed only as a land where outlaws roamed, useless or wasted land, and then a place where people ran and raffled land. Oklahoma, for some, is forever stamped with visions of oil rich prosperity, poverty stricken people in dismal shanty towns or overburdened jalopies heading west to escape the Depression.

Life in Oklahoma has often seemed based on the whims of fate, with Prosperity and Want often serving as two sides of the same decision making coin toss.

Although filled with progress and still evolving

today, at the start of the 20<sup>th</sup> century, it was struggling to bring some sense of definition. Just what was the nature of this land and its peoples? What was this crazy patchwork of cultures forming, often in spite of itself, into a single quilt of unique strength and beauty?

We tend to like to find prototypes in history to serve as role models and as reflections of our better selves. They often give voice to values or dreams we hold dear. They can reflect the aspirations and hopes of a time, a people, or a place. When daily life becomes too boring, mundane or placid there is always the vicarious adventures of someone else to add what is missing. We enjoy these stories and want to see ourselves reflected in them.

Despite the preponderance of biographies of great men and women, however, it is the common person who constructs history. Occasionally some person will (by accident or intent) rise above the whole to achieve passing honor or notoriety. They can give voice to an issue, express what others cannot and share wisdom learned. It is impossible, however, for a single voice to define an entire group. Multiplicity of voices, experiences, and values bring needed balance to the historic image.

Much of early Oklahoma storytelling was considered 'rustic' and of such a common style that it was easily denigrated as uncultured or coarse. As the oil boom of the twenties brought new status, state newspapers reveal a deep awareness in American society of "class." This was based firmly in race, ethnicity and economics.

For Oklahoma of the mid-century, hastily trying to distance itself from its Dust Bowl image, it was often doubly important for some to turn away from the 'simple' folkways in favor of acquired social polish. Suffering from a cultural inferiority complex due to its late entry into the Union, the setbacks of the Depression and other issues, Oklahoma was especially focused on being seen by outsiders as modern, progressive, and refined.[2] Not until the national bicentennial in 1976 did there emerge any serious attempt to reintegrate these particular 'folk' customs back into either a state or national conscience.

To understand a society, one must come to know and appreciate, all the layers and dimensions expressed through all the folk stories, wisdoms, and legends. This produces the most multidimensional

---

[22] Edwards and Ottaway's *The Vanished Splendor: Postcard Views of Oklahoma* series, and other sources, show the often awkward and self-deprecating caricature images of the frontier and pioneer days of early 'Frontier City' (an Oklahoma City amusement park) and the often over eager booster ads of the early days of statehood.

topography of a people. Thus, while some might prefer a certain type of story or specific style of telling, without that necessary diversity, understanding of the stories is compromised. To use the quilt analogy, it is seeing one block to the exclusion of the whole work and failing to grasp how they work together to create beauty.

**THE STAGE AWAITS, THE LIGHTS ARE
DIMMED, AND THE AUDIENCE
FRIENDLY...**

# CHAPTER 1

# ORIGINS

*Stories give us history*

*and stories make us strong;*

*Stories give us meaning ;*

*They show us right from wrong.*

*Stories open eyes, minds, and hearts;*

*Stories help us end;*

*Stories help us start.*

*Stories keep our all our secrets -*

*They set our feet to roam;*

*Stories ground us and guide us back home.*

*Stories make us laugh, cry, and see;*

*Stories help me see you;*

*Stories help you see me.*

Storytelling is an art form both ancient and contemporary that is brought to vibrant new life with each generation. Societies around the world, and for a variety of motives, utilize the oral art of storytelling. The sharing of stories has been the primary means of communicating community standards, teaching sacred values, sharing cultural knowledge, and remembering history.

Numerous works have explored the use of oral storytelling among indigenous groups in Oklahoma but less has charted the development of storytelling in modern Oklahoma history. The lingering influences of the Victorian and Edwardian eras, with their emphasis on virtue, sought to find an ideal life free of the negative forces of their day. Out of that ethos arose the use of literary based works of classic history and literature to instill 'culture' in children that was used widely in the classroom and the library. This was pivotal in preserving the art form even as it often constrained it into rigid forms.

Nationally, storytelling received a renaissance as several things happened in close conjunction, as the nation prepared for the Bicentennial everything from candle making to weaving became popular skills to reacquire. Additionally, the innovative 'Foxfire' project further encouraged people to learn from community elders the skills, knowledge and wisdom that were on the verge of dying out.[3]

In the 1970's in Jonesborough, Tennessee, the first storytelling festival began a renaissance of the traditional art form. This set in motion, a multi-decade re-discovery of the dynamic entertaining, educational, and transformative communication art form known as 'storytelling.'

When the term "storytelling" is used today it is often through a lens of preconceptions: storytelling is for children, storytelling is synonymous with a lie or tall tale, storytelling is unsophisticated, storytelling is boring, etc. A further layer of misconceptions clouds the lens: storytellers will be reading to an audience, storytelling is what writers do, storytelling has to have a purpose beyond simple entertainment, and storytelling is what cinematographers do.

As noted earlier, for the purpose of this work a common definition of the art is used. Storytelling as an oral communication or narrative is a rather wide umbrella.[4]

To further define and identify various means employed, the following have been selected. One

---

[3] The Foxfire project began in 1966 in Rabun County, Georgia and is preserved today as The Foxfire Fund, Inc. at http://www.foxfire.org/

[4] Oral storytelling in this work refers to the *art of sharing stories or anecdotes through speech (oral communication) for purposes of entertainment or education.*

who reads a book to children or audiences is a "Story Reader." The person who learns and shares a story using the basic skills of oral communication is a "Story Artist." The person who shares, often in small, intimate settings, amusing anecdotal stories using the basic skills of oral communication is a "raconteur." The one who integrates aspects of theater arts (music, puppets, drama, etc.) into the learning and sharing of a story using oral communication is a "Story Performer." The individual who follows a cultural tradition as to form and content (such as medieval stories) or uses ethnically specific styles and stories is a "Culture Bearer" or "History Keeper." Various cultures may also utilize specific titles or designations that can further clarify the scope of their work in sharing stories.

Regardless of style, all are "storytellers" but these classifications provide a more precise descriptive pool for explaining what a specific artists' expertise or focus is based on specific skills and behaviors. They may also, hopefully, help to provide guidance to those who talk about these artists or who attempt to understand as programmers and event planners just what the artisan will bring to their event.

In a similar manner the stages of a storyteller's artistic development often offer many challenges to those within the telling community as well. Just how long, for instance, is one a novice? When is one a master teller? Are there stages between the two ends of the spectrum and how does anyone know they have migrated from one level to another? All of these are important issues still waiting serious contemplation and widespread adoption within the craft.

A general tool to provide a rough understanding might be a simple rubric. A simple rubric or spectrum may open dialogue and assist storytellers in deciding where they are in their development and help them map out their own skill building and training. Some possible starting places for the discussion might include the designations listed here.

NOVICE - Person enjoys listening to stories told but may not yet have told a story in public. A person who is first a listener or new to storytelling. They may know no stories, a few simple tales, or have been sharing stories for only a brief time. They may have learned the basics of storytelling and story structure (beginning, middle, and end).

BEGINNER - A few stories to share, little public telling experience, attended 1-5 workshops or classes, and are still learning. Begins to identify story types and explores new skills. May have told to groups or in intimate settings. This "training wheels" stage is a place of exploration in small but gradual steps.

APPRENTICE –A person who has learned and shared a few stories (5-10), has attended concerts, workshops (5-20), and has begun to explore more challenging aspects of story selection, delivery, and stage skills (used for any presentation before an audience). Demonstrates growing confidence in delivery. Explores and understands the various forms of storytelling to identify their strengths and appreciate the art in other styles.

STORY COLLECTOR / TRAVELER - A small treasure chest of stories have been collected, polished through workshops and hearing others tell, and made personal through multiple telling experiences. Goal criteria may be to develop a larger store of stories (20-50), shared in 20-50 public concerts, programs, had varied story experiences, able to teach others basic techniques, have developed some specialized telling ability, still learning.

ARTISAN - Greater wealth of stories to share, have done many concerts, programs, and share stories with great skill. May conduct workshops ; able to teach skillfully basic to intermediate level classes; have developed a highly personal style and ability; have explored other arts and experimented with merging them with storytelling or explored ways to expand skills and delivery in new and innovative ways. A person who has learned many stories for a variety of age groups, topics, or settings. A person who has had experience sharing stories before a variety of audiences. A person who has developed, or crafted, their own stories for sharing. A person who has gained more knowledge and training in the use of stories for specific themes, the use of props and other additions. A person who has begun to address the needs of other aspiring artists through workshops or presentation on the art and skills of storytelling. A person whose story delivery and stage presentation will be confident, capable, engaging and skilled.

MASTER:  A wealth of stories, publications, recordings, or experience in many venues, frequently cited/quoted, able to teach others more advanced techniques, skillfully presents storytelling as an art form, highly developed general and specialized ability/style. Adds to the philosophical and artistic understanding of storytelling as an art form through mentoring, writing, teaching; still learning. A person who has wide experience in telling, learning, and teaching about storytelling arts.  A person who creates their own stories, adds to the resources for other story artists and builds the storytelling art community.  A person who discovers, encourages and acts as mentors to new aspiring story artists.  A person recognized by their peers as being an artist of unique value, skill, and talent.

These are my individual terms but hopefully, they may begin a dialogue among story artists toward a more intentional understanding of development and advancement within the art form and to provide journalists and others with greater understanding of the layered complexity of the storytelling art form and its diverse artists.  They can also help to bridge the understanding gap about how storytellers learn, improve, and are understood by others.

Marilyn A. Hudson

# CHAPTER 2

# INFLUENCES

Marilyn A. Hudson

# CHAPTER 2

# INFLUENCES

Oklahoma's cultural and artistic influences are varied. Numerous native groups as well as a variety of European traditions all contributed to the culture that emerged. The nature of storytelling – and its strength through time - is that it adapts and evolves through a process of fluid and responsive cultural exchange.

The following are mere signposts directing attention to the merging currents of storytelling in the developing region we know today as Oklahoma. They are representations of vast, and sometimes uncharted, territories of research.

The rich heritage and ongoing use of storytelling in Native American cultures has been addressed through numerous dissertations, articles and books. Less explored have been the use of storytelling within other ethnic groups in the state (African-American, Asian and Hispanic). This work will focus on its presence in various institutions (libraries, schools, and religious centers).

**Te Ata.** Her name meant "bearer of the morning" and her stories brought the dawn of a new era in the appreciation of the traditional arts in the life of Oklahoma.  In the 1980's, she was named Oklahoma's first cultural treasure and it was fitting.[5] She is a recognized artist of the state and of her people, the Chickasaw.[6]  A recent stage production was developed that honors this remarkable woman. One of the stories she often told, "Baby Rattlesnake", was later adapted by another noted Oklahoma storyteller and author Lynn Moroney into a popular children's picture book.[7]

She was an innovative artist who believed that "art binds all people together."[8]  She tried to bring people together through all of her artistic endeavors and to expose the humanity that connects all groups. It is fitting that an auditorium on the campus of Oklahoma University of Arts and Sciences honors her. Numerous books, articles, and documentaries have chronicled her life and work.[9]

---

[5] Roger Harris.
http://digital.library.okstate.edu/encyclopedia/entries/T/TE001.html
[6] "Heritage".  The  Chickasaw  Nation,  at
http://www.chickasaw.net/site06/heritage/250_951.htm
[7] Lynn Moroney at
http://www.ipl.org/div/natam/bin/browse.pl/A212
[8] Te Ata
http://www.usao.edu/teata/storyofteata.htm

[9] See http://www.usao.edu/teata/whatsnew.htm;
A book also covers her life.
http://search.barnesandnoble.com/Te-Ata/Richard-Green/e/9780806nces

**The National Storytelling League**. In 1903, a group meeting of teachers and interested individuals in Tennessee formed what would become The National Storytelling League. Support for the goals of sharing the best of literature and the oral tradition spread and by 1908 events are being in various states.

Education in this time period was one of the most influential agencies at work in society. Guided, in part, by the philosophical groundwork of John Dewey, education was seen as crucial to social advance, betterment, and civilization. "… *through education society can formulate its own purposes, can organize its own means and resources, and thus shape itself with definiteness and economy in the direction in which it wishes to move.*"[10]

**Hearth-Side Tales**. A newspaper article from Norman, Oklahoma details the events of a "Hallowe'en Party" held at the Blake home. Among the party activities included a contest for the telling of the "most thrilling" ghost story and the best performances on the string, music, and recitations.[11]

This simple story illustrates the core hub of story preservation and continuation in the twentieth century. Storytelling was rooted in the home. That was where stories were first heard, learned and shared. In that setting was heard the fairy tales and

---

[10] John Dewey. My Pedagogic Creed. *The School Journal*, (Vol. LIV, No. 3) January 1897.
[11] "Hailowe'en Party." [sic] *Norman Democrat* (Oct. 27, 1905).

folktales of the parents. In that intimacy people absorbed the family stories, legends, and tall tales of family and their community. This early inculcation of story was then nurtured and refined in more formal settings of classrooms, church schools, libraries and other cultural centers.

# CHAPTER 3

# CLASSROOMS

# AND

# LIBRARIES

"Storytelling" in the twentieth century has evolved to mean many things. Described as the writing of a book, the reading of a book aloud, the acting out of a book's story, the creation of images to convey a story line, and the process of orally conveying a story, the flexible terminology can be confusing. It is entertainment, it is a folk art, and it is theater. This flexibility of definition has resulted in more than a little confusion by journalists, publicists, the general public, and even the storytelling community itself.

Oklahoma City, like many growing cities in Edwardian era America, had an active collection of communal societies and groups. In 1913, a Mrs. Bussington hosted a meeting of "Circle No. 4" of the Oklahoma City "Twentieth Century Culture Club."[12] On the agenda was a presentation by Dr. Dora Martin on the topic of the stories best told to children.[13] It may be assumed other communities, as they grew, also incorporated similar activities into

---

[12] The "circles" were smaller groups within an organization and served to allow members within a geographical area to develop activities and relationships thus often expanding the reach of an organization and creating a 'circle' of friends. These were usually women's organizations and could be found in both civic and church groups.

[13] Oklahoman (April 9, 1913):4.

the lives of their local families.

In 1914, the President of the "Story Teller's League of America", Dr. Thomas Richard Wyche came to the state. He was one of the lecturers at the state normal school in Edmond, now known as the University of Central Oklahoma. Assisting in this storytelling course was a Miss Marie Hofer of Chicago. The audience for these specialized courses, according to the newspaper accounts, were superintendents, teachers and other educators.[14]

Modern components of every library or classroom "story time" are "picture books" where images move the story forward. Since the 1800's books had been illustrated with random scenes or added pages of noteworthy classical art related to the book topic. Picture books, however, did not come to be readily available to parents, libraries, or schools until much later in the twentieth century. As a result, most libraries and schools in the early years of the twentieth century first provided youth literary experiences using oral storytelling.

In this process, the finest of noteworthy writing was adapted, or memorized, to share with audiences using the traditions of the storyteller. Even later, when picture books were more common, some librarians and teachers continued to use oral storytelling and served to preserve the art form in the

---

[14] Oklahoman (June 14, 1914): 11.

face of newer competing entertainments.

Driven with near missionary zeal, some local libraries saw it as their purpose to elevate the literary level of their communities and in doing this to improve the community as a whole. Many communities in this era were resistant to a concept of a library as a free and equalizing resource. Some libraries were resistant as well. However, spurred by the rationale promoted by Andrew Carnegie that libraries should be open to all, accessible by all and even by children, the emergence of children's services soon developed.[15]

As the libraries neared 1920, children's programming was a standard but was also subject to funding shortfalls. The Carnegie Library of Oklahoma City, however, did not allow a lack of budget to hinder outreach to community children. Mrs. Edith Barrows Russell provided a regular story "feast" in 1915. The effort garnered some three hundred children in attendance at one program. Russell described them as being from "comfortable", or middle to upper class, families. The support of this sector of the population was appreciated, and the library was often dependent on the generosity of the more wealthy of the society, but Russell was apparently not content.

Attendance, Russell felt, numbered too few of

---

[15] Library: An Unquiet History, Matthew Battles, 2003 ; History of Libraries in the Western World, by Michael H. Harris, 1995.

the "newsboys" and children whose only entertainments were found on the streets. Her motivation was a hope to expand the library work among that group of children.

Where adult book clubs and studies merited inches of columns noting all the socially prominent in attendance, this was not the case with many of the children's programs. Events in the newspaper were often merely mentioned in only the broadest terms of a children's time or program. Occasionally, more details were offered. Such as the fact that in an August 1915 event, a Mrs. Ren F. Davis shared *Uncle Remus* tales. [16]

The reports in the capitol city newspapers might be used as an indicator of what was happening elsewhere in the state. As children's services gained in value to the community it might be assumed this emphasis on the oral tradition of literary tales was one actively used in other locations.

Evidence of a guild of The Story Teller's League[17] is found in Norman in 1916.[18] In Edmond in 1917, a summer school included courses by Alice Justin Jenkins of Chicago. As a representative of the National Story League, she provided two weeks of

---

[16] Oklahoman (August 29, 1915):5.

[17] Although many forms of the name appear in the various articles they all refer to the National Story Teller's League formed in 1904 in Tennessee.

[18] "Summer School well Attended." Oklahoman (June `8, 1916):15.

lectures in storytelling. [19] This indicates that through public education storytelling was benefiting the lives of state children.

In 1917 the children's librarian at the main library in downtown Oklahoma was Mrs. H.B. Carter. The program of the August third "Story Telling Hour" reflects a standard methodology used by many schools and libraries. The day's program completed a series on the tales and legends of Spanish history and was led by Carter and an assistant, Miss Muriel Rummel.[20]

Schools and libraries were active in the use of storytelling as a vital tool in communicating fine literature, cultural knowledge, and entertainment. They were not, however, the only groups utilizing the art form.

In March of 1919, the Oklahoma Sunday School Association held its convention in Oklahoma City. A featured part of the event was the presence of Mrs. Nannie Lee Frayser of Louisville, Kentucky. She was dubbed "perhaps the best teller of Bible stories in the United States." Frayser was to be a featured speaker and leader of the children's programs of the convention. [21]

Storytelling had definitely found a home among children and educators but storytelling was not

---

[19] Oklahoman (May 20, 1917):35.
[20] "Storytelling Hour." Oklahoman (August 3, 1917): 57.
[21] "Storytelling" Oklahoman (Feb 17, 1919): 4.

limited to the very young. Although often viewed as telling lies, or simply being a waste of time similar to early attitudes towards 'play party' games and music, storytelling was also shared among adults. Informally, and not labeled as such, professions and social groups continued to share the tales of previous generations, local history, and local legends. Among cowboys, railroad workers, miners, and farmers folk storytelling continued as an accepted part of their work culture. [22]

In 1921, the Story Tellers League in Norman was "reorganized" during summer school. Leading the first meeting of the group was storyteller Helen Ruth Holbrook. Subsequent meetings selected officers: Jean Beisher, Elizabeth Phillpin, Miss Ida Z. Kirk, who was an instructor in speech and also the group sponsor. The agenda of the group was learning and sharing stories, legends, and exciting real life adventures. [23]

The positive and expansive tenor of society was brought to a halt by the events of October 1929 that thrust America into an economic decline due to the crash of the stock market. Fortunes were lost overnight. One of the results of this process was a collapse of many of the social institutions of previous days. The social clubs often served the community elite and the rising middle class. Although some clung stubbornly to a world that was, in the thirties

---

[22] Metropolitan Library Folk Collection.
[23] "Story Tellers Form Club at University." Oklahoman (July 5, 1921): 4.

there were fewer of these clubs actively reported in most newspapers. Changes, however, were at work in the broader society to bring storytelling into the spotlight.

In 1943, nationally syndicated columnist with the Oklahoman, Edyth T. Wallace, queried if storytelling for small children had become a lost art. 24 Noting the changes since the ready access of children to books, she urged parents and others to see that it did not disappear. To curb the loss, she recommended a book and a brochure she had found to provide tips for learning and sharing stories. 25

In the post war years, the emphasis was more on 'storytelling' in its literary and cinematic terms. There was still use of the term as a synonym for lying – or stretching the truth - as seen in a story from 1954 from Anadarko. A local native leader, Robert Goombi, in response to claims that Gallup, New Mexico had a larger native population, the work of a "*Gva pol.*" This was word said to be Kiowa for a "big storyteller."[26]

The Toastmaster's organization in the mid-

[24] Edyth Wallace entry, Women's Hall of Fame, Oklahoma State University Library, accessed at http://www.library.okstate.edu/oralhistory/owhof/inductees_alpha.htm#Wlink (June 29, 2012).
[25] Wallace, E.T. "Is Storytelling for Small Children Becoming a Lost Art?" The Oklahoman (Jan.14, 1943:6).

[26] "Anadarko Tribesman Debunks Gallup claim to Indian Capitol." Oklahoma (July 30, 1954):30.

decade named a Mrs. I.E. Yakoushkin as storyteller.[27] The local Oklahoma City parks department included storytelling in its summer activities for children and youth.[28] In 1953, young Martha Clifton was noted as a University of Oklahoma student who was sharing storytelling and drama as a play supervisor for the Oklahoma City parks department. [29]

Community cultural centers varied by community. Generally even smaller towns could count on the local school, church or library being a partner in all things educational or literary. Local church workers in 1954 Oklahoma City had the opportunity to learn new story sharing skills, and hone those already used, in a workshop held in the main library community rooms.[30]

A column in the local Oklahoma City newspaper, "Uncle Ray's Corner" encouraged history with each entry. Discussion of ancient Roman or Grecian history were often prefaced with a common statement such as "the old storytellers said" and this may reflect a philosophy of the time about the role of storytelling in society. It may also

---

[27] "Club to Meet on Wednesday", Oklahoman (March 28, 1956):8.

[28] "Dance Day at Friday in Parks", Oklahoman (July 21, 1953): 3. ; "Parks Plan for youngsters" Oklahoman (Nov. 5, 1959):47.

[29] "Summer Time and the Living is Easy". Oklahoman (June 28, 1953)41.

[30] School Leaders to Attend", Oklahoman (April 16, 1954):47.

reflect the manner in which storytelling was utilized in an earlier generation as seen by the literary emphasis often employed.[31]

A more novel use of the concept of storytelling appears in 1951. It does indicate the level that storytelling as a concept was enmeshed in the common culture. A small, grainy graphic showed a scantily clad Little Red Riding Hood and a leering Big Bad Wolf. It was advertised as the "Bedtime Story Review." The adult only dance and dine event featured the unspecified "talents" of "Suzanne", "Joy Doyle", and "Les Moore." The music for the evening was provided by "Al Tell and the Storyteller Band."[32]

Except for aberrations such as the entertainment provided for adults by the sex starved Wolf and Little Red, most storytelling was seen as a suitable entertainment for youth while the theater, the cinema, or the concert hall were designed to appeal to more discriminating adults.

It can be assumed adult informal storytelling continued in the form of casual in-home story sharing, work-place talk and in similar settings even without any direct evidence. The popularity of storytelling among children remained a constant even in the face of growing access to television.

"Story time starts at City Libraries" declared one

[31] "Uncle Ray's Corner" Oklahoman (May 7m 1956): 31.
[32] "Bedtime Story Review", Oklahoman (May 16, 1951):61.

Oklahoma City headline in 1965. It described a "spring storytelling cycle" being readied by the local library system. In the early sixties, the city libraries had announced a goal of increasing library use and identified storytelling programs as one of the means to achieve their goal. When summer reading programs were announced they had twin objectives of sharing books and sharing stories. [33]

The local libraries may have been influenced by the highly successful work of storyteller-librarian Augusta Brown in New York. Contextually, however, it was sometimes unclear if the meaning was storytelling or the reading aloud of a printed book to a group of children. [34] The next year, however, in "Libraries Slate Storytelling" it is made clear that Oklahoma City children would be given opportunity to "listen to the centuries old art of storytelling." The implication was that it was focusing more on the oral tradition. [35]

Even locked library doors could not halt storytellers from sharing with children in the Del City Library in 1966. The new library was part of a larger recreational facility combining other activities into a single structure. In August of that year it was still a few weeks away from formal opening but the

---

[33]

[34] "Storytime Starts at City Libraries" The Oklahoman (Feb.9, 1965: 26).

[35] "Libraries Slate Storytelling" The Oklahoman (Jan. 25, 1966: 38).

program was given.[36] That same summer storytellers from the library system appeared at the Capitol Hill branch. The artists there included: Mary Ann Wentroth, (Children's Services Coordinator), Beatrice Manus (Children's services Librarian at Capitol Hill), Diana Lingle (Main Library) and Wilna Tipps (Del City Children's Services Librarian).[37]

A reoccurring anchor of storytelling was the classroom. Just as early teachers used storytelling to improve their own communication skills and to entertain students, later teachers would also see its potential. Today, many formal education professional groups recognize the value of the art of oral storytelling in their work with students.

In 1972, Claire Jones conducted a workshop on "Creative Dramatics and Storytelling." Jones was the head of the speech and theater department at Oklahoma City University in Oklahoma City. Jones went on to develop several significant theater arts programs that enriched Oklahoma City. 38

Storytelling found a regular home in Oklahoma, as elsewhere, in the annual summer break programs

---

[36] "Closed' Sign Doesn't Affect Use of Library.' Oklahoman (Aug.18, 1966)45.

[37] "Closed' Sign Doesn't Affect Use of Library.' Oklahoman (Aug.18,1966)45

[38] First Workshop Today" The Oklahoman (Sept. 30, 1972: 7).

offered through local public libraries. 39 A delightfully productive symbiotic relationship emerged through the annual summer reading focus. Local libraries saw increases in circulation that validated their usefulness in their community. The reading programs, blending reading with creative arts and performances (serving as reward and impetus to library use), created a win-win scenario.

While delighting children everywhere, storytelling was also being rediscovered as a viable and entertaining pleasure for adults. In 1973, the now famous Jonesboro Storytelling Festival in Tennessee was born proving that storytelling had a wider appeal than just for the nursery set.40

It had proven itself entertaining to a wide age group, but it was also being suggested by academics that storytelling could be useful in many disciplines. In an AP story by George W. Cornell in November of 1973, Harvard theologian Dr. Harvey Cox expressed the need for theologians and the church to reclaim storytelling. 41

The local library system of Oklahoma City, the

---

[39] "Libraries Sets Special Events for children." The Oklahoma (June 2, 1972: 37).
[40] "History of the Festival" at
http://www.storytellingcenter.com/festival/history-fest.htm
[41] "Christianity Needs To reclaim Storytelling". The Oklahoman (Nov. 23, 1973:94). Cox went on to write numerous works that explored the folkways of various religious groups.

Metropolitan Library System, continued its annual
"storytelling workshops" at three libraries that
repeatedly served as hubs in the 1970's and 1980's
for such events. Those hubs included Southern Oaks,
the Downtown library, and the Ralph Ellison branch.
Presenters at these training events included Roxanne
Rhodes, Donna Deniston, Karen Jones and others. In
1977, the MLS was even actively "looking for
storytellers" to be trained to learn "book selection,
storytelling techniques, and theme ideas" for
preschool story times in area libraries.42

Into the 1980,'s storytelling continued to be
encouraged and promoted at Oklahoma City
University under Claire Jones and in public libraries
as well as retirement centers. 43  The convergence of
the re-discovery of the art form through the folk
revival and the national bi-centennial resulted in a
new interest in traditional and innovative
storytelling.

In Oklahoma City this meant an integration of a
group of emerging state artisans and a new emphasis
on the arts as being important to the state's overall
quality of life.  The result was that people were being
drawn to storytelling from a variety of fields and this
meeting of talent would set the stage for a time of

---

42 "Libraries Looking for Storytellers." The Oklahoman
(Aug.19, 1977:22).

43 "Retirement Home Plans Storytelling as Regular Activity."
The Oklahoman (Aug. 3, 1982: 42).

great organization and forward momentum within the state.

In 1982, Linda Levy, along with the OKC Arts Council, the Metropolitan Library System (MLS), and other groups combined to launch a "storytelling festival" event aimed primarily at adult audiences. Thus, the direct ancestor of "WinterTales" was born. A year later, Levy, along with Lynn Moroney of the OKC Arts Council were sharing stories in a multi-arts venue called, "Festifall."

Ann DeFrange, noted local journalist, in 1986 interviewed visiting storyteller Bob Wilhelm, a featured teller at that year's "WinterTales." The focus of the event was to revive "our native skills to communicate to other people."[44] Oklahoma City, along with other parts of the state, however, had been involved in reviving this particular skill for a number of years.

The groundswell of a storytelling renaissance emerged from the folk music movement in the early 1960's. The approaching national bicentennial, when all things in the communal past were revisited and re-discovered, also saw a revival of many neglected "folk arts." Storytelling was one of those.

Forward momentum was also encouraged with new developments in the storytelling art world. The

---

[44] "Storytelling Art Form Worth Keeping Forever." The Oklahoman (Jan. 26, 1986: 96).

Jonesboro Storytelling Festival provided an impetus in the 1970's. This event and the response to it proved storytelling was not a lost art and had the power to draw large audiences. The development in 1988 of "Tellabration!", or an "evening of storytelling" would further move the art of story into new arenas over the next two decades. [See entry on the history of the event in Oklahoma).

Some segments of Oklahoma society needed little effort to "discover" or "rediscover" storytelling. They had kept the flame of custom burning in their own cultural milieu. Oklahoma's rich palette of ethnic groups included Asians, Native Americans, Europeans, and African-Americans. This meant that a vital, often untapped and sometimes unappreciated, treasure of knowledge, instruction, and history were just waiting to be discovered and shared. In 1996, Tulsa based Muscogee Indian, Wilburn Hill noted he had been brought up to be a tribal storyteller. All such individuals enriched all of Oklahoma as they shared stories and revealed the important role of the storyteller in society. The storyteller often entertains but also preserves history and serves as ambassador for cross-cultural communication.

Memory of Storytelling in School: *"I remember we crowded into the library at my school. This storyteller was there. I remember he wore these colorful suspenders, you know the kind to keep pants up, and this wild bow tie. It was almost too big for his neck! Usually, I was pretty bored at things we did at school. That day, though, hey, he opened his mouth and I don't think I blinked or moved until the teacher was leading us out to go back to the room...."*

Memory of Storytelling in a Public Library: *"This lady came to our library. It was a dinky town and the library pretty small so it was pretty exciting when we had this 'storyteller lady' come! She was so nice and when she started to tell the stories it was like she talked to just me. I felt important; special, you know..."*[45]

---

[45] Anonymous.

# CHAPTER 4

# GUILDS AND GROUPS

One formal early group, as noted previously, was known simply as the "Story Teller Club." They were apparently related to the National Storytelling League. Identified locations for this particular group include Oklahoma City, Norman, and Ponca City. No evidence of other statewide clubs or groups has been found until the early eighties with the formation of The Territory Tellers.

According to early member, Letty Watt.: "With the help of Lynn Moroney from the Arts Council of Oklahoma, Roger and Marie Harris, Rosemary Czarski, and others we organized the Territory Tellers, early in the 1980's, holding regular meetings, conducting workshops around the state and telling stories on every stage we could find. I was the first President of Territory Tellers, and enjoyed every story we shared. By then, Texas had an annual storytelling festival and Oklahoma began with a spring stage at the Arts Festival until moving to Wintertales."

Collaborating with the Oklahoma City Community College in 1987, the group presented a special concert and dinner program. Although the news piece named no tellers, the public was assured they would "weave stories of our great states' beginnings."[46]

Other leaders of Territory Tellers serving as President and board members have included Vance Morrow, Connie Fisher, Lois Hartman, Steve Kardaleff, Sam McMichael, Barbara McBride-Smith, Bob Bjorklund, Rosemary Czarski, Bonnie, Smith, Karen Bray, Darla L'Lallier, Elizabeth Parker, Roger Harris, David Holder, Garland McWatters, Chester Weems, Gordon Greene, Theresa Black, Salley Riffey, Barbara Fisher, Roxann Grissom, Marilyn A. Hudson, Molly Lemmons, Tina Saner, Shaun Perkins, Greg Rogers, Jeannette Harjo, Phillip Harjo, Stella Long, Valerie Kimble.

Utilizing the promotional experience of member Rosemary Czarski, the organization saw its events covered in local news frequently. A 1991 press release raised awareness of the organization in "Storytellers Band Together." The piece encouraged anyone interested in the preservation, sharing or listening to this art form, to become a member.[47]

Not all story clubs, beyond the early National Story Tellers League groups mentioned earlier, are known. The following communities, however, all had storytelling groups active at some point during the later 20th century and the first years of the 21st

---

[46] "Oklahoma Territory Tellers Dinner Theater." Oklahoman (February 1, 1987): 86.
[47] "Storytellers Band Together." Oklahoman (Dec. 29, 1991):58.

century.

Ardmore. *Word Weavers* operated under leadership of librarian-storyteller Valarie Kimball.

Bartlesville. *Tallgrass Tellers*, under leadership of professional teller, Fran Stallings.

Choctaw. *Wayword Tellers*, under leadership of Rosemary Czarski, Susie Beasley, and Liz Parker.

Lawton/Apache. Steven Kardaloff and Sam McMichael kept the torch of storytelling thriving in southwest Oklahoma through groups and events.

Mayes County. *Mayes County Storytellers*.

Midwest City. *Wayword Tellers*, under leadership of Rosemary Czarski and Susie Beasley.

Norman, *Norman Storytellers*, under leadership of Marilyn A. Hudson. Also, *The Norman Story Circle*.

Norman. *Word Weavers*, OU, under leadership Tim Tingle and Greg Rogers they introduced students and campus to storytelling.

Oklahoma City. *Boomer Storytellers*, Toastmaster's, continuing a tradition in the organization dating at least to the 1950's, operated under leadership of Marge Smith.

Oklahoma City. *OKC Tellers*. Facilitated by Marilyn

A. Hudson. The group's goal was to promote, train, and encourage storytelling and story listening in the greater Oklahoma City region.

Oklahoma County. *Oklahoma Association of Storytellers*, facilitated by Marilyn A. Hudson, Molly Lemmons, Kathryn Thurman and Barbara Wright Jones. The group's goal was to promote and train intermediate and semiprofessional tellers.

Tulsa. *Tulsey Town Yarn Spinners*, under leadership of Connie Fisher, Darla L'Allier and others.

The Territory Teller's from its origins was committed to the idea of encouraging new talent. The "Storytelling 101" workshops offered around the state were designed to introduce the basic skills of oral storytelling to interested audiences. Given the wide range of appeal and use of storytelling target groups have included churches, youth leaders, educators, business people, health care workers, early childhood teachers, community leaders, parents and librarians.

# CHAPTER 5

# EVENTS

Throughout the history of storytelling the art and public venues traveled in comfortable companionship. The Roman writer Horace observed that there had been many famous before Agamemnon but that they are "unwept and unknown, because they lacked a sacred bard."[48] Markets, fairs, festivals, harvests, and celebrations all brought the skills of the storyteller into public view. Audiences, then as now, were delighted by the stories of great heroes, clever people, magical worlds and romantic adventures.

As with many art forms, storytelling had a ready home among family, friends, and small community groups in the state from earliest times. Formal storytelling "events" seem to have appeared in Oklahoma first in public library programs for children. Occasionally an event occurred with storytelling included. Nationally, however, a widespread revival of folkloric customs occurred just prior to the Bicentennial and with that renewal of interest in the art form other venues emerged.

---

[48] Horace. The Works of Horace Translated Literally into English Prose. Translated by C. Smart, available online at The Gutenberg Project at http://www.gutenberg.org/files/14020/14020-h/14020-h.htm

**Festivals: Some Early Miscellaneous Venues.**
As early as 1926, The Oklahoma City parks
department included storytelling in its roster of
summer programs for youth.[49] Through the next
decades, the art would remain a vital ingredient of
summer activities for city youth.[50]

In 1973, Beaver's Bend near Broken Bow, was
the site of the Kiamichi Owa-Chito (a term meaning
big hunting trip). Many name musical performers
were listed as well as other activities and artisans,
including an unnamed Choctaw storyteller.[51]

In Enid, the National Speech Festival, came to
the Phillips University in April of 1976. This
competitive event included a category of "American
Storytelling" as a way to celebrate the Bicentennial
of the United States. Participants were from Arizona,
California, Arkansas, Colorado, Illinois, Kansas,
Louisiana, Missouri, Texas, and Oklahoma. Stories
shared in the competition had to be 3-7 minutes and
classified as either social or historical.[52]

---

[49] "Recreational Center to be Open Monday." Oklahoma (June
20, 1926): 30.
[50] "Dance Day at Friday in Parks", Oklahoman (July 21,
1953): 3. ; "Parks Plan for youngsters" Oklahoman (Nov. 5,
1959):47.
[51] "Forest Festival to be Held at Beaver's Bend", Oklahoman
(13 May 1973) 210.
[52] "Phillips to Host Speech Festival." Oklahoman (April 9,
1976):72.

City Parks Programs. Almost any community of size across the state tried to provide some entertaining and educational activities to address summer boredom and reduce juvenile delinquency. The Parks department, often in conjunction with other community groups (churches, schools, civic groups) would set a schedule, gather volunteers and arrange planned activities for neighborhood children. In 1951, Oklahoma City provided among their offerings "storytelling hours." It is unclear, however, if this was traditional oral storytelling or if it was simply reading from a printed book.[53]

**Oklahoma City Arts Festival.** On many occasions storytelling groups or individuals were provided an opportunity to participate in the annual spring arts festival.

Memory of the Arts Festival: *"One year they had put the storytellers in this big canvas tent. If there is one thing you can count on is that it will rain during the arts festival. They had placed a small stage, a microphone and tables and chairs on one side and in the opposite corner they had put in a small beverage bar where people could get sodas or beers. The people I was with sat down at one of the tables and began listening as the storytellers told their stories. They were good too! Then people began to drift in to visit the bar. Suddenly, almost*

---

[53] "Dance Day Set Friday in Parks." Oklahoman (July 21, 1953)3. This article is also a stark reminder of how things were once with its notice regarding special times and places for African American children.

*drowning out the performers, was all this "Clink. Clink." as used bottles were tossed in this recycle bin and "Talk. Talk" as all these people visited. Then a big delivery truck arrived and sat with its motor humming away. We inched our chairs up until we were practically in the storyteller's lap! The tellers just laughed and talked louder. I guess you have to be able to handle all kinds of unexpected things at those events..."*

**Wintertales.** Lynn Moroney is recognized as one of the founders, along with Linda Levy and others, of *WinterTales* in 1982. She is recognized too as the force behind its subsequent development. Her role as advocate for the event, and her crucial partnering with the various funding sources and arts councils, cannot be minimized. In the midst of a general artistic convergence, diverse opportunities were generated. In this period, the leadership of the storytellers in Oklahoma and the several local arts communities, all moved closer together to work in mutual benefit. As a result, there was a growing appreciation of storytelling in the community and an awareness that Oklahoma might have something unique to offer as state tellers found their voices.

The events where local storytellers gained crucial experience and exposure as artists included numerous occasions on both the local and state levels. "Storytelling '83" was labeled "A Family Festival" and was held at the Oklahoma Theater

Center.[54]

Center.[54]   A unique "Liar's Contest" was used to hook audiences in 1983. Sure to be a crowd pleaser, it was uniquely promoted through special invitations sent to notables in Oklahoma City.   Despite numerous contacts to various local politicians and leaders, however, only a few were courageous enough to respond.  Those who joined the festival tellers were some very popular local television personalities: sportscaster, Bob Barry Jr. and meteorologist, Rick Tesatano.[55]

In 1985, the storytelling festival after moving around the calendar from spring to summer to fal,l finally came to rest.  Unnamed planners suggested that storytelling, with its historic roots in tales shared over long winter nights around the hearth, was best suited to the winter months. *Wintertales* was born.

Wintertales, thrived and in its fourth incarnation, its program focused on stories and music of the medieval era.  It opened with a reception featuring music, book displays related to the time from the local public libraries, and dance demonstrations by the International Folk Dance troupe from the University of Oklahoma. The national tellers featured for the event included Laura Simms, Gloria Timpanelli and myths and legends from members of the state organization, The Territory Tellers. In addition, the event shared stories with over a

[54] "Professional Storyteller to Perform", Oklahoman *June 26, 1983):100.
[55] Chris Brawley. "You Won't Believe This One." Oklahoma (July 4, 1983): 1.

thousand local school children and a hundred professionals in a three day program.[56]

Ann DeFrange, Oklahoman staff writer, in a 1986 longer article introduced the concept of storytelling, its value, and told a little about the artists who would be performing.[57] The guest tellers were nationally known artists Robert Wilhelm and Syd Lieberman. Lieberman was quoted as indicating he was looking forward to hearing uniquely Oklahoman tales because he called the memory of such shared stories "a gift."[58]

The state organization for storytellers, The Territory Tellers, shared the stage with Lieberman in an afternoon concert.[59] These "Oklahoma Olio's" were primarily designed to showcase the emerging talent of Oklahoma storytellers in partnership with the arts council event. This shared stage concept was beneficial to the emerging state artisans and contributed to the understanding of the voice of Oklahoma to national and international traveling professionals. Over the years, the best of the working storytellers from Oklahoma and its statewide story organization performed in the

---

[56] "Storytelling Fete Harks Back to Medieval Days".
Oklahoman (Feb.1, 1985): 54.
[57] Ann DeFrange. "Storytelling Art Form Worth Keeping Forever." Oklahoman (Jan. 26, 1986)96.
[58] Ann DeFrange. "Storytelling Art Form Worth Keeping." Oklahoman (January 22, 1986): 96.
[59] Price, Mary Sue. "Stories to Light Up light." Oklahoman (20 January 1985):107 ; "Winter Tales", Oklahoman (26 January 1986 )97.

spotlight of the historic and unique Stage Center.[60]

The unique building of Stage Center had begun life as a new theater for the successful Mummers Theater troupe of Oklahoma City. The architect was John M. Johnson, a member of the "Harvard Five," a group that developed to counteract the often soulless forms of modern style. His unique vision was a modern sculpture structure inspired by electrical circuitry. The response to the unique design was one of extreme love or hate for the abstract aspects of cubes and tubes. Many saw the underlying sense in the futuristic structure and others merely saw architectural anarchy. In some ways, however, it was an apt reflection for the arts in Oklahoma. Marked for demolition, the site was where many talented Oklahoma story artists shared tales as diverse and unique as the state they represented. [61]

At the conclusion of the 1987 event, the festival was featured on the social pages. A reception was given to express appreciation to all the storytellers and volunteers. Hosted by the library system's Friends of the Library group the committee included: Mary Ruth & Leo Mayfield, Betty & Edward Gregory, Mona Lambird, Nancy Allen, Sandra

[60] As of the writing of this work, the Stage Center is due to be demolished and corporate offices to be built in its place.
[61] For additional information on the history of Stage Center see Steve Lackmeyer's "Stage Center Doomed?" Oklahoman (July 27, 2013)6C and Brianna Bailey's "Final Curtain Call: Stage Center supporters call for Last Hurrah." Oklahoman (Dec. 29, 2013)1c.

Austin, Mary Nichols, Howard McKinnis, Arvon Staats, Charlotte Norman, Jean McLaughlin, Carol Furrow, Jacque Long, Kay & Bob Armstrong, Sarah Woodward, and Janet Mann.

Featured artists for the event were national tellers Jim May, and Fran Stallings. Local artists were Marie and Roger Harris and John Hinkle. Sponsors for the event were The Arts Council of Oklahoma City, National Conference of Christian and Jews, the Metropolitan Library Friends, and Oklahoma City Community College.[62]

In the early years of the event, a strong partner was the Metropolitan Library System. Staff volunteered at the event and libraries promoted the it to their customers. The libraries, already a solid supporter of storytelling in their children's services, were a natural partner in promoting and sharing this art form. In assuming a supportive role they continued a relationship with storytelling that could be traced back to the early days of their first library provided through a Carnegie gift.

Over time, as funding sources and continuing education needs rose, the event evolved to include numerous workshops to attract teachers and

---

[62] "A Reception Thank You." Oklahoman (February 11, 1987):50; see also a 1989 reception event to 'honor the storytellers and sponsors' but none of the photos appear to show the storytellers or the sponsors but only musical groups. "Reception Honors Festival Participants" Oklahoman Feb.1, 1989)25.

performers. It was looked forward to by many such professionals throughout the region and, despite inhospitable weather occasionally, it was highly valued. It was the one of the major training venues for emerging Oklahoma storytellers for all of its life at Stage Center in Oklahoma City.

In the later nineties, the state storytelling organization hosted each year a reception for performers, guests and volunteers after the last evening performance. In the reception hall of Stage Center, its dome shaped ceiling glittering with tiny white lights, the sense of story magic lingered and was a fitting setting for the time to meet and mingle.

The presence of the state group in the event shifted over time    from sharing the stage with featured tellers to a lunchtime "Pails and Tales" and an "Oklahoma Olio." This last was a free concert featuring members of the state organization and was offered late in the day at an awkward time and sometimes was left out of publicity materials. [63]

For the next twenty years, the home of the annual event was primarily the modernistic Stage Center facility on Sheridan Avenue in downtown Oklahoma City. The facility was in the early years the heart of the growing arts community in Oklahoma City and reflected a growing national trend away from simple community art centers to a more professional approach to theater arts.

---

[63] Interview, Storyteller M2, 11/12/2012.

The Oklahoma City Arts Council announced in 2009 "Winter Tales" was at an end. In its place, local arts leadership would reach back to reclaim a name used decades earlier, the Oklahoma City Storytelling Festival. Like its predecessor, it would feature multiple tellers, performers, workshops and family matinees.

Memory of Winter Tales: *"I remember the lounge in the Stage Center – all gray and cave like – where we always headed for lunch and the 'Pails and Tales'. It was a lot of fun to see old friends and listen as person after person told stories. There were newbies and experienced alike. Some newbies, you could practically hear their knees knocking together! Workshops where I learned a lot every year. Then the concerts and the olios…I was always so sorry when it was all over and I had to go home."[64]*

**Encyclo-Media.** Noted international teller David Titus recounts that for a decade storytelling was a vital part of this educational event held in Oklahoma City and the metropolitan area. The purpose of the event was to connect school library programs, educators, and vendors for continuing education. The first one occurred in Edmond in 1981. Over time the event moved to the Myriad Convention Center (now the Cox Center) in downtown Oklahoma City.

"When I came to Oklahoma … Encyclo-media

---

[64] Anonymous.

had its first event. At the second one, I suggested to Barbara Spriesterbach that the librarians did not have anything to do on Thursday evening and were shy about going out or trying to connect with someone else. We started a Storytelling-Round-Robin. It was held in the hotel and refreshments were served."

Titus also noted the rationale for introducing storytelling to the event. "It was to encourage others to tell a short story and just have something to do. Some of the "real." storytellers started and then others jumped in. It was amazing to see someone shine that had never told outside of their school library or family. I moderated it for at least 20 years. Many people looked forward to it as one of the highlights of Encyclo-media."

As other events, started happening on Thursday night it was moved to the lunchtime in the convention center." He indicated that others moved in to moderate it and it eventually, like the Encyclo-Media format itself, simply. [65]

**Oklahoma "Tellabration"(R)** --"Tellabration" is a global celebration of storytelling held each November. Storytellers around the globe celebrate storytelling in evening concerts in homes, halls, fields, theaters, bookstores, schools, and any place they can share their love of the art form. In 1988, a storytelling guild in Connecticut decided to offer a special evening of storytelling. It proved so

---

[65] Interview, David Titus, Feb.4, 2013.

satisfying that they planned more and soon they were happening all over the country.

According to one source, Oklahoma's first "TELLABRATION! (R)" was in 1992 at the Sooner Theater in Norman. Local educator Letty Watt, also an active storyteller, served as producer.

Some other producers through the years have included: Bob Bjorkland, Lois Hartman, Fran Stallings, Lynn Moroney, Rosemary Czarski, Bonnie Smith, Marilyn Hudson, Steve Kardaloff, Sam McMichael, Beth Kouba, Liz Parker, Shaun Perkins, Jeanine Harjo, ....

Many Oklahomans contributed their talent to sharing stories in the state's many events of "Tellabration!" Usually these professional and semi-professional artists told without fee in order to share their art.  Sometimes, ticket sales provided guilds with important funds to support their art and sometimes they collected donations for local shelters, food banks, and other community programs.

Some of the story artisans sharing at these events included: Ginger La Croix, Letty Watt, Theresa Black, Robert and Marie Harris, Barbara McBride-Smith, Patsy Packard, David Titus, Weckeach Bradley, Randy Silver, Jared Aubrey, Bob Bjorklund, Lois Hartman, Kris Hunt, Peggy Kaney, Sam McMichael,  Jo Etta Martneay Bryan, Whit Edwards, Debra Garnejkul, Connie Fisher, Vance Morrow, Sky Shivers, Steve and Pat Kardolff, Will

Hill, Tina Saner, Emilea Moring, Sally Riffey, Kathryn Thurman, Marilyn A. Hudson, Chester Weems, Rosemary Czarski, Liz Parker, Bonnie Smith, Jeannette Harjo, Stella Long, Shaun Perkins, and others.

The Pioneer Library System in Norman, Oklahoma, hosted the 2002 event. Featured tellers were Lynn Moroney, Jahruba Lembeth, Michael Corley, Maureen McGovern and Marilyn A. Hudson.[66]

In 2003, Oklahoma State Representative Danny Morgan, Garland McWatters then president of the state storytelling group, and storyteller Bonny Smith, asked then Governor Brad Henry to designate a week of storytelling. As a result, November 16-22, 2003 was named as the "Oklahoma Tellabration Storytelling Week!"

Storytelling," Morgan said as he shared the proclamation to an audience in Prague, "is a valuable method of sharing American folklore and is an important means of contributing to Oklahoman's knowledge of the history of our state."

A Memory of Tellabration: *"You just can't compare one Tellabration to any other. No way. Each once is like a snowflake. One of a kind. Unique. I remember one in an empty store at 50 Penn Place, one at Oklahoma City Community College, one at*

---

[66] "Library to Host Tellabration Event." Norman Transcript. Nov.15, 2002, A9.

*Southwestern Christian University, at the Norman Library and the Choctaw Library. There was one in a home one time as well! All so different but all of them filled with wonderful stories and great storytellers."[67]*

**Storytelling 101 – Territory Tellers.** The state storytelling organization, The Territory Tellers have been committed to making storytellers during their entire existence. They organized with a two pronged mission of preservation and perpetuation of the art of storytelling. To do that they have offered beginning and intermediate storytelling workshops and programs. Some of the venues have included"

**Sun Fest (Bartlesville).** Locally known story artist Fran Stallings, joined by members of the Tulsa storytelling guild (Tulsey Town Tellers) provided a story concert and learning time for many years at the Sun Fest event. Members of the Territory Tellers would meet for a lunch, stay to share tales, and linger to listen to others share.

**Red Earth Festival.** This world class festival celebrates North American Native cultures and brings tribal members and tourists from across the nation. The event is famous for its dancing and art exhibitions. Storytelling has been a key feature since its inception. Gifted artisans have also shared their craft in local schools and in local venues such as

---

[67] Anonymous.

public libraries as part of this festival.

**National Storytelling Festival in Oklahoma City.** The national storytelling organization emerged in 1973 in Jonesborough, Tennessee as NAPPS (National Association for the Preservation and Perpetuation of Storytelling). In 1994, the group changed their name to NSN (National Storytelling Network) with membership spanning the nation.[68]

In 2004, the annual conference of NSN was held in the Cox Center in Oklahoma City with events being held in several other venues as well. Through partnerships with The Territory Tellers, the Metropolitan Library System, the Oklahoma Arts Council, Oklahoma City Arts Council and others, the conference brought in storytellers and introduced Oklahoma to a new level of story presence and accomplishment.

**Spirit of Oklahoma Storytelling Festival.**[69] Nancy Lenhart Matthews prepared a narrative chronicling the history of the festival sponsored by The Territory Tellers. *"The "Spirit of Oklahoma" Festival is relatively an infant in the storytelling world. This year, 2013, will be its seventh year in existence...*

*A few years back Territory Tellers (TT) as*

[68] "Our History," National Storytelling Network, website, http://www.storynet.org/about/index.html accessed 1/29/13
[69] Jim Etter. "Festival To Present history from the Heart." Oklahoman (may 13, 2007)23A.

*Oklahoma's largest statewide storytelling group bid to have the NSN conference in Oklahoma City, Oklahoma. They were chosen for this honor and for two years worked to bring storytellers from all over; a conference that would be not only rewarding but fun for all. Many hours of hard work from all the TT members accomplished what they had set out to achieve. After the conference, everyone was tired but elated that it had gone so well. All the hard work had paid off and many rewarding and pleasant memories lingered for all those who had worked to pull it together.*

*After recuperating from this task, someone suggested they try giving a festival. They knew they could do whatever they set their minds to do; after all, they had hosted the NSN conference. So the board and members of TT went about putting together a festival. Several members living in the Seminole area had worked with the Seminole College. When the college was approached, they were willing to help and a bond began to form. Next, the city of Seminole embraced the TT organization and they were on the way to the makings of a festival.*

*Everyone had fingers crossed and breaths held at the first festival[70]. When it was over a collective breath was let out and everyone knew they had to continue with this wonderful thing called "Spirit of Oklahoma' Festival. Evaluation sheets had been passed out and ideas for the next year started to form*

---

[70] The first festival was held June 2, 2007 in Seminole, Oklahoma. Territory Tellers Tattler (Winter 2007).

*almost immediately. Each year seemed to bring more ideas and people wanting to know about this wonderful thing called storytelling. Workshops for beginners, intensive workshops for experienced tellers, concerts, and story swaps, even classes that would give the participants CEU were on the program. Before they knew what had happened it was a growing, educational, and fun event.*

*Seminole residents began to expect to see the faces of TT members throughout the year when they met with the Chamber of Commerce, city officials, and college officials. Businesses in town began to put signs in their windows and even participated with promotion of the event. The neighboring town of Prague even started to participate. Prague has a Kolachi festival and elects a queen. They are known for this Polish sweet pastry filled with fruit, meat or cheeses, the kolachi. The elected queen and her court came in costume to the festival as greeters on the Saturday of the festival and donated kolachi's to the delight of all.*

*In the third year, TT was advised it would be the year to tell whether the festival would succeed. The festival committee put their heads together to make it the best yet. They enlisted the expertise of storytellers who had helped with festivals in their own states. The college arranged to give credits for a class taught the evening before the festival began. Advertisement of CEU credits for certain workshops given by national tellers were a definite plus. Members donating their time on the radio, writing grants, enlisting the help of the Seminole community and the Seminole College and members of the national storytelling community worked hard to make that third year a winner.*

*Fourth and fifth years kept letting them know the impact storytelling has on a community. Surrounding communities in the vicinity began asking to participate; colleges began recognizing stories aren't just for kids and can have a definite value for different areas of the college curriculum (English, Writing, Speech); and businesses and cities began working together through the storytelling event. The fourth year they had audiences from 30 towns in 21 counties in Oklahoma, and 9 towns in 6 different states (Arkansas, Texas, Louisiana, Missouri, Kansas, and Georgia.)*

*In the fifth year the motels were so booked that TT members had to enlist surrounding towns for accommodations. In the future TT is looking to take the festival to other towns due to requests to bring this event to other communities. Next year (2014) will see the festival with a new look and hosted in Bethany, OK. "* [71]

**Choctaw Storytelling Festival (2004).** Noted storyteller and graduate of OU, Tim Tingle organized the CSF.

---

[71] Lenhart, Nancy Matthews. "History of the Festival", 1/22/13.

A published statement cited that in May of 2004, Tingle founded the Choctaw Storytelling Festival. It was a three-day celebration of "Choctaw narrative: traditional, historical, and personal."

It goal was a joining together of tribal elders with youthful attendees and sought to "promote the ongoing transmission of foundation stories so critical to the Choctaw community."

Stories were told in the Choctaw language as well as English, according to Tim Tingle.    It was held annually at the McAlester Choctaw Community Center, 1636 S. George Nigh Expressway from 2004 to 2009.  Another event, Choctaw Nation Labor Day Festival in 2012 included storytelling as part of the entertainment but no performers were named.

Storytelling, like many other art forms, evolves and tries new things.  One of the major innovations of the late 20th and early 21st century is the "Story Slam."    This is a competitive storytelling on a specific pre-posted theme.  Hopefuls will put their names in a container ("the hat") and if their name is drawn they have to share a timed story. It is appealing with young audiences and is often part of 'open mic' nights at colleges, clubs and other urban activity centers.  They can be fast paced and raw, much like their cousin, the poetry slam.

**OKC Story Slam.** -- This event was born from the fringe experiences of the National Storytelling

Festival held in Oklahoma City. The format was a growing one seen in urban centers across the country and featured a combination of traditional storytelling, open mike, standup comedy and the raw energy of the poetry slam. Storytellers placed their names in a hat and if the name drawn was theirs, the teller had a few short minutes to tell a story. Winners were selected at the conclusion of the event by those attending. Settings could be cafes, shops and museums. The Istvan Gallery, 1218 N Western, Oklahoma City hosted many "story slams" while Tulsa's event found a home in a popular night spot, the ENSO Bar.

Molly O'Connor recalls the genesis of this event in Oklahoma City: "My first real job right out of college at the ripe age of 24 was with the Arts Council of Oklahoma City and included coordinating the WinterTales Storytelling Festival. While I had grown up in OKC and had attended the Festival of the Arts, Twilight Concerts, and Opening Night multiple times, I had never even heard of this event that was presented by the Arts Council, (which by the way had been rated by USA Today as one of the top 11 Storytelling Festivals in the country!). In my first year, I was bewildered by it and had to hit the ground running with the plans. It wasn't until after I made it through my first WinterTales that I really could grasp and appreciate the world I had stepped into...the world of storytelling.

The irony is...I had been around great storytellers my entire life. I recall sitting on porches outdoors in Denver during cool summers and listening to the great aunts and grandparents recreating past events and characters, lively and funny, but also deep and heroic. I recall the "Jumpy, Roly and Coo-Coo Stories" my Dad would create and tell as my brothers and I would listen and laugh at the edge of the day's end. They were usually stories of the three vivid monsters defeating Mr. Jones, the Watermelon salesman and getting into all sorts of chaos, usually at the ice cream store. I recall my mom giving tours at the Harn Homestead to visitors from all over the world. My imagination ran wild with images of the Harn family staking claim and building their lives on the bizarre and open horizon of early statehood....just two blocks from where my head hit the pillow every night. The best teachers I had in school always used story to convey the message, whether it was history, math, science or English.

It's really occurred to me that I have been around great storytellers my entire life. In fact, I feel like my own life is a quilt of stories, stitched together randomly, yet serendipitously.

WinterTales sanctioned something I had always known as familiar and normal into a true art form. I loved organizing the events and appreciate that I got to add my own creative ideas to WinterTales. What I remember about WinterTales is the people who came to the event year after year. They were like a close-knot family, truly "salt of the earth" people, and WinterTales was kind of their family reunion. I loved getting to go to Jonesborough, Tennessee every year for the International Storytelling Festival. It was there I got to spend hours listening to all of the most amazing professional storytellers and think about who I wanted to hire to come to Oklahoma City. I stopped wearing mascara when I went to the festival because I was either crying from some of the heart wrenching stories people told...or the hilarious ones...or some that were just so beautiful and inspirational.

The storytellers were kind of like celebrities, but also very humble down to earth people. I have some fond memories of just hanging out with the storytellers, laughing into the late hours of the night. I cannot think of any other community that I connect with on a spiritual level as I do with the storytelling community.

So, one thing that occurred to me when I was working on WinterTales is that I was in my 20's and most of the audience was my parents' age. What a shame, I thought, that more people my age weren't attending WinterTales. Where was our future audience?

At a storytelling convention, I ran into some other young people and learned about new efforts to make storytelling "cool" and appealing to younger people. I learned about storyslams and fringe storytelling events as well as storytelling events that focused on the LBGT community or the stories from people of color. Then, I heard about the Moth[72]...and I began tuning in. I was hooked.

So, what do you do when you find a great idea you like? You copy it. With minimal resources and good community partnerships, I launched the first OKC StorySLAM at the Untitled Art Space in OKC. It got good response, and it continued...and thrived! It had a regular following. It brought together diverse voices. It was often very campy, but I think the best sign of success is that after the program was over, people would stick around and talk...often to people that they had not known before the slam. I literally saw complete strangers connect through a story.

The OKC StorySLAM has changed and evolved over the years. It eventually moved to the Istvan Gallery in OKC. As an organizer, I like the randomness and suspense of the event. You rely on people to show up and sign up to tell. You have a theme and rules (stories must be seven minutes or less), and somehow it all kind of works. I actually love the surprise element of the storyslam. You never know who is going to get up and tell. It's very quirky. People from the audience will sometimes listen to a few stories and then just get up and tell something improv-style. Those are often some of the best stories. As someone raised Catholic, I would compare the storyslam to a sort of communion: different perspectives, but same theme. We all leave

---

[72] "The Moth" at http://themoth.org/about

fulfilled and with better understanding of our fellow humankind.

I love all art forms. But I think there is something about storytelling that is so accessible and powerful and life-changing. Some of the most moving stories I have heard have not been rehearsed and developed works of art from professional storytellers on a stage...they have been from ordinary people in line next to me at the grocery store or in the seat next to me on a bus.

There is something so universal about storytelling. There is something about it that is so transformational. And I believe that there will be an increased need for storytelling in the future. As technology advances and our world becomes smaller, I believe people will be hungry for authenticity and the ability to connect with fellow humankind. What can connect people better than a good story?"

**Tulsa Story Slam** – Co-Producers of the event are Branda Jean Piersall and Michelle Sisemore Bias. They launched out into the world of the storyslam recently and it has, like the Oklahoma City event, attracted attention. In recounting the history of the event Piersall remarked, "....early last year I tried to get The Moth[73] to come to Tulsa to start hosting story slams. They were less than enthusiastic, said maybe with enough signatures we could get them to come in

---

[73] "The Moth" at http://themoth.org/about

a couple years. Tulsa is definitely in the middle of an artistic and downtown revitalization, so I certainly didn't want to wait 2 years to get something this interesting going. I asked a friend, Michelle Bias to join me in organizing monthly events, which we have been doing since March of 2013. Our following is growing and we will host our first yearly "Grand Slam" in April where all the previous month's winners come to tell a story for the (all in fun) title "Best Storyteller in Tulsa." Each monthly event is so good, some are very touching and personal, some are just plain hilarious with all the crazy true stories. There just isn't anything like it, and it is a fun and interesting and different thing to do on a night out.[74]

**Tapestry of Tales: Tulsa's Storytelling Festival** – April 2014 saw Tulsa hosting a festival through a partnership of Boston Avenue United Methodist Church, Oklahoma Center for Community & Justice, and Phillips Theological Seminary. Featured performers such as Donald Davis, world renowned North Carolina Appalachian storyteller; Corinne Stavish, a Jewish teller; Tim Tingle, a Native American teller, and Charlotte Blake Alston, an African-American teller.

**OKC Storytelling Festival** -- In a press release from 2009 came an important announcement. "The Oklahoma City Storytelling Festival, formerly known as the WinterTales Storytelling Festival, has

---

[74] Information from Branda Piersall ; see also
http://www.oksotulsa.com/ and
https://www.facebook.com/oksotulsa/info.

a new name and new season, but will continue the 28-year tradition of entertaining adult audiences with imaginative stories and performances."

Now held in the fall, the Oklahoma City Storytelling Festival was launched September 11 and 12 at Stage Center. *"After much planning, volunteer co-chairs Phil Carlton and Kym Koch Thompson promise a weekend full of entertaining stories from world-famous tellers Kevin Kling, Susan Klein, Motoko and Minton Sparks.*

*"Everyone should go for the simple fact that a single person on a bare stage can hold an audience spellbound for hours without any visual aids – just their voice painting a vivid, compelling picture in your imagination," said Koch Thompson, who has been volunteering for the storytelling event for five years. "Storytelling is an art form that easily creates connections and communities of people by offering life lessons or shared experiences. No matter whether the story covers common or uncommon ground, the listener can always relate to it because the art is in the telling," she said. With four renowned tellers of different backgrounds, adult audiences are sure to relate to their colorful, humorous and inspirational stories.* [75]

In 2013, the downtown area was in disarray due to several major street projects and planners shifted

---

[75] Press Release, Oklahoma City Arts Council, 2009.
Permission to reproduce provided by Peter Dolese, 1/29/13.

the event to the History Center.[76] The new location was an ideal one providing escape from the often oppressive heat of late summer in Oklahoma and an easy to reach location with ample parking. It was, in many ways, a match made in heaven and reflected a creative merging of entities with great potential.

**Ghost Stories.** -- No group of tales is as old as the ghost story. Homer in the 8th century B.C.E. inserted encounters with the ghosts of those long dead into his famous poems. One of the oldest 'true life' haunting comes from ancient Rome, so it no mystery that ghost stories are a favorite genre to the storyteller and listener.

In the 1990's, the Oklahoma Historical Society launched a series of fall events to showcase the state's major historical sites at Old Central in Stillwater, Fort Washita at Madill, Overholser Mansion in Oklahoma City, Fort Gibson, and the George Murrell House in Park Hill. Significant historical sites everyone. They also shared another unique characteristic in having legends of haunting associated with them.

This series of 'Real Ghost Stories' began in 1992 and by 1997 actor and re-enactor Steve Abolt of Texas was leading candlelight night walks at Ft. Washita. Professional storyteller Marie Harris was also then returning for a sixth spooky year to the Overholser Mansion. At Ft. Gibson similar tours

---

[76] "Storytelling Festival Moves to Oklahoma City History Center." Oklahoman (August 16, 2013)7D.

were enjoying the talents of professional storyteller Bea Wright of the Tulsa Town Tellers.[77]

Oklahoma City's famed Overholser Mansion was a particular favorite. The lovely 1904 gothic style house lent itself to tales of ghosts and the mysterious. Donated, with all original furnishings intact, to the city the house was recognized a place retaining more than memories of past residents. For many decades ghost stories were not openly promoted. Times, interests and needs for upkeep can change what is seen as proper. In the later years of the 20th century and the first decade of the 21st this alternative interest in history was recognized and used as an effective fundraising tool. Either through use of professional storytellers, or docents, stories of legends, myths and haunting filled the mansion for in recent decades.[78]

---

[77] "Historic Sites Offering Halloween Ghost Tales." Oklahoman. (Oct. 19, 1997):427; Penny Owen, "Thrill, Chill to Tales at Four Legendary Haunts", Oklahoma (Oct. 28, 1999):15"Ghoulish Tales to be Told" Oklahoman (Oct. 22, 1998):3.

[78] Ann DeFrange. "Haunting Stories to Fill the Mansion", Oklahoman (Oct. 25, 1992):237; "Mansion Scares Up Ghost Stories", Oklahoman (Oct. 17, 1993) p. 93, featured Marie Harris; Karen Klinka, "Haunting Options." Oklahoman (Oct.23, 2003)17 Edmond, showing Teresa Black; "Tour a Haunted Mansion", NewsOk.com ; "Tour A Haunted Mansion", October 2010, online news at http://newsok.com/tour-a-haunted-mansion/article/3506047.
Storyteller was Marilyn A. Hudson. Hudson performed for four years at the mansion but most publicity found was through

Some of the tellers known to have shared tales multiple times at the mansion include Marie Harris, Teresa Black, Nancy Singleterry, and Marilyn A. Hudson.

Over the years concerts, festivals, and other events included ghost stories. Even groups unfamiliar with the storytelling art form enjoyed tales of historic Oklahoma haunts and legends. One example is from 2008. A *Paracon* (paranormal conference) sponsored by various ghost hunting groups was organized by Tonya Hacker and Tammy Wilson. It was held in El Reno at the old Elks Lodge and a professional storyteller, Marilyn A. Hudson, as "The Ghost Teller", shared tales. Also on hand was Oklahoma TV personality John Ferguson, aka "Count Gregore", and Enid author and academic, Brian N. Young aka "Dr. Fear." All shared stories, local legends and historic tales suitable for the occasion.[79]

**Special Touring Programs.** As the statewide organization, The Territory Tellers, faced the

---

alternative media such as "Wimgo", the "Oklahoma Gazette" and various blogs, websites or in-house flyers.

[79] David Zizzo. "Convention Spot Lights the Unconventional". Oklahoman (March 20, 2009)18A.; Featured storyteller was Marilyn A. Hudson, "The Ghost Teller"; also present were Oklahoma TV personality, John Ferguson aka "Count Gregore", Enid author/academic , Brian N. Young aka "Dr. Fear."

centennial of the state, a special touring program was developed that showcased the multi-cultural history of the state. *"History From The Heart"* was a troupe of female storytellers. The company included Liz Parker, Bonnie Smith, Molly Lemmons, Stella Long, Barbara Jones, Susie Beasley, Jeanette Harjo, and Kathryn Thurman.

The stories, often shared in historic or cultural clothing, combined to portray women from the tellers' own families who had helped build the state. Although few of the women of the stories could be found in any history books, they were a vital part of its past, and they all reflected that great Oklahoma spirit.

A few years later, another group of tellers Molly Lemmons, Kathryn Thurman, Susie Beasley, Marilyn Hudson, and Barbara Wright Jones united. *"Casting Strong Shadows"* was set at a community event and wove engaging, funny, inspiring, and honest stories together in a fun framework. The intent in these stories was to honor positive role models in life. Drawn from many time periods and cultures, the stories told were of strong hearted men and the positive influence they cast over their families, their communities, and their world.

Another troupe that toured was **Stories2Go.** It was comprised of with storytellers Molly Lemmons, Barbara Wright Jones and Marilyn A. Hudson. They traveled in central Oklahoma and shared stories at various senior and community centers.

# CHAPTER 6

# GETTING

# THE WORD OUT

P.T. Barnum, the famous 19th century business man, said that "without publicity something terrible happens – nothing." President Lyndon Johnson on signing the National Endowment of the Arts act remarked on the crucial role the arts have in society:

*"Art is a nation's most precious heritage. For it is in our works of art that we reveal to ourselves and to others the inner vision which guides us as a nation. And where there is no vision, the people perish."*[80]

Publicity, and promotion of storytelling events and artists, is then a crucial aspect of encouraging the arts. It is a practical necessity, as well, for the success of business related to the arts.

Based on the press coverage found in local papers, the decade of the eighties was a good one for the art form in Oklahoma. Numerous in-depth articles discussed the art form, newspapers reprinted pieces from national periodicals, and everywhere there seemed to tremendous before and after coverage of events and people. Many of the articles,

---

[80] Found on "Performing Arts Convention"
http://www.performingartsconvention.org/advocacy/id=28;
"Legacy for Leadership", National Endowment for the Arts at
http://arts.gov/sites/default/files/Legacy.pdf

by comparison to more recent examples, carried reporter by-lines.

During the next decades, this rich promotion faded from view in many of the larger newspapers and other media. This might have been due to the trend to segment the periodicals into specific regions of the community (with 'North' or 'West' versions targeting events only in those regions) and rising production costs in general.

As the community grew along with costs the number of event stories also became more numerous. As a result many newspapers were truncated. Also, newspapers were often no longer produced in the community further diminishing the potential for local promotion of events.

The persistent misconceptions of the art form as being suitable only for children may have played a role as well. This may be reflected in the cycle seen from the late seventies to the first decade of the new century. It may also reveal a dissonance, or tension, in popular understandings of what constitutes art and how storytelling fits into that matrix. Whatever the causes, as the millennium turned, the amount of news coverage for local story art groups and the art form generally diminished.

In retrospect of the century, announcements of events started out as mere notices in the general events columns. Then they progressed to a more prominent place with the growth of such things as

"Wintertales" and "Tellabration!" by late century.

Heading toward the new millennium, storytelling events were again reduced to brief calendar listings without fanfare or details in many newspapers.[81]   In a 2006 article, Molly O'Conner, Winter Tales director noted that despite the festival being held for over twenty years, many still were surprised at hearing of its existence.[82]   This, despite the fact it was one of the best advertised, and longest running, storytelling events in the state of Oklahoma.

According to several artists interviewed, one of the issues continually faced by the art form has been it's perceived as solely an activity for children. This narrow view has labeled storytelling of minimal artistic or general value. It is not a new idea because in some of the earliest feature articles concerning Wintertales, that aspect was part of the discussion by producer, Lynn Moroney, storyteller Fran Stallings[83]

---

[81] "What's Going On?" Oklahoman (Nov. 22, 191):47 labeled the Tellabration event without using the term and merely called it a storytelling festival. "What's Going On? Oklahoman (November 17, 2001):83 Norman Tellabration; "Calendar". Oklahoman (Nov. 17, 2003):20, Midwest City event: "Weekend Look", Oklahoma (Nov. 11, 2005): 2D, Mayflower Tellabration.

[82] Brandy McDonnell. "By Word of Mouth." Oklahoman (February 20, 2006): 1B.

[83] Fran Stallings. "  "The National Storytelling Journal Spring/Summer 1988, accessed at http://healingstory.org/the-web-of-silence-storytellings-power-to-hypnotize/

and others.[84]

The evening of storytelling, Tellabration, while not an Oklahoma innovation, was readily embraced in order to restore the balance and share stories for and with adult audiences. It sought intentionally to fight the tendency to categorize the art form solely as something for children and to awaken audiences to the dynamic and empowering value of storytelling to address adult needs. In the process bringing together even the most diverse community stake holders. One storyteller had this to say: "We fragmented storytelling into kids' stuff and adult stuff. The adult stuff had value but not the kid's stuff. As a result, we had stand-up comics without any soul and children's stories without any grit. Stories have to go the life span...we build on them. Foundation, first floor, second story, and attic – they all have to be preceded by something else or they fall down and it is the same with stories in our life. "[85]

Reporters, educators, and public often confused the act of reading of book to children as the art of oral storytelling.[86] It was a common complaint of

---

[84] "Author to Stress Need to Read." Oklahoman/Norman (March 2, 2001)5. Storyteller Marilyn Hudson was described as being there to "read stories."

[85] Name withheld by request. Interview dated September 4, 2010, Oklahoma City.

[86] "Storytelling Nook", Oklahoman (Nov. 24, 1993):50 showed "storytelling Shirley Pritchett" reading a book at an MLS event; "Storyfest Set for Zoo", Oklahoman (July 16, 1999):86, featured readers from Barnes and Noble: Interviews, Storytellers B, R3,M1.

storytellers in the later twentieth century that news articles said they would be "reading" to their audience. This was assisted by a common tendency for educational resources dealing with books, reading and retelling of written stories to all be labeled "storytelling." Educational conferences saw many books, puppets, programs and activities all labeled as 'storytelling' tools for the teacher. It was a prevalent enough misconception that noted storyteller Fran Stalling commented on it in an Oklahoma City article from 2006.[87]

One negative side effect of this lack of promotional coverage is that local artists are often hard to identify. Although the state organization consistently focused on encouraging, training, and providing opportunities to emergent talent they reflected only a small portion of active storytellers in any given time period. Many active and emerging artisans functioned outside the state arts council, state arts groups, or any long-standing local guilds. Too often, the storyteller's name was totally missing from programs or news articles. For some events the names may be forever lost and that is a loss to the artistic history of the state and of storytelling in general.

At the root of much of this invisibility may be a too narrow definition for the art of storytelling. Anne Pellowski in her classic history of global storytelling, *The World of Storytelling* (originally published in

---

[87] Brandy McDonnell. "By Word of Mouth", Oklahoman (February 2, 2006):1B.

1977 and updated in 1995), identified the myriad forms the art used. Storytelling could be folk art, literary art, performance art and much more, combining in fascinatingly complex patterns of creative work.

This diversity allows many different types of performance styles to enrich the art form:

- Traditional tellers who share their stories quickly in a conversational style,
- The teller who emphasizes the rustic values and customs of the heartland
- The teller who reflects the styling and mannerisms of urban centers
- The tellers who mix music/dance and stories
- The tellers who uses the best of the world's literature as their source
- The teller who carries on the traditions of their culture
- The tellers who blend story telling with traditional theater arts
- The tellers who blend innovative and stylistic manners, movements or delivery into their storytelling

Despite their different approaches and methods to the story process, they all reflect the essence of the art form of oral storytelling.

As communication and social interactions have changed over time, so has the manner in which information about storytelling events has changed.

As noted, one of the most significant changes has been the diminishment of coverage for local storytelling activity through local media (newspapers, radio and television). As the sheer number of alternate activities has grown in most communities the news worthiness of story events has sometimes been minimized. Springing up to fill the void have been social networking sites, online event and community calendar sites, and free online pages. All such promotional outlets are inherently limited since they only reach those who use those mediums.

Recent trends in marketing have been a high level of customization of advertising and news. Highly focused, and individualized, approaches provide a challenge of getting the word out about story events. The need to reach across market niches and into new potential audiences becomes crucial. Add into that hurdle the common misunderstandings about what is meant by "storytelling, what audience or age will be interested in storytelling, and, well, the future should be very interesting when marketing the art form.

# CHAPER 7
# STORYTELLERS

Prefacing many of the entries in this directory of artisans are quotes collected at one time from the peers of the storytellers and their listening audiences.[88] These remarks are identified through quotes and italics. While unable to gather information from all significant performers, a deep appreciation goes to all of those who so generously, and graciously, responded to requests.

This list can only be a small fraction of the many storytellers who have shared their imaginative work with audiences large and small. The people profiled here represent the broad spectrum of storytellers who have enriched modern Oklahoma. They range from transplants to home grown, from apprentice to master teller, and from those who specialized in one form and those who explored diverse interests.

---

[88] A thank you to all those performers who so graciously responded to requests for interviews or with information and details about their work in Oklahoma. It was the goal of the author to be as inclusive of styles, cultures, and mediums of artists as possible. Some information was gathered from records and correspondence in the collection of the author (bio sheets, flyers, etc.).

It is the challenge of this author that others will seek out and record the histories of the mentors and role models of their corner of the state. Add them to the roster of the trail blazers who captured imaginations and taught people the power and beauty of words.

**Al BOSTICK** – Albert Bostick Jr. (Mr. B., Mr. Al. or Mr. Albostick {kids sometimes say it as one word}), has been a storyteller for more than twenty years, a career that started as an artist-in-residence with the Oklahoma Arts Council. Bostick hails from New Orleans, Louisiana, and has long had an interest in the folklore of Africa and African-America.

He attended Grambling State University and holds a Bachelor of Arts Degree in theatre, with emphasis in acting/directing. He has also attended the University of Oklahoma has completed Masters work in the field of drama.

Bostick has worked with numerous Oklahoma theatres including: Oklahoma Shakespeare in the Park, the Pollard Theatre of Guthrie, the Black Liberated Arts Center, and Oklahoma Children's Theater. While working with the Oklahoma Children's Theatre, Bostick wrote and directed, *At The End of the Rainbow, There's Only Rain...,* and *Anansi the Spider*. Later, he was twice invited to set the show for the St. Louis Black Repertory Theatre where he also later wrote and directed *The Adventures of Brer Rabbit*. These shows toured throughout St. Louis public schools.

As an Oklahoma Artist-in-residence, Bostick has performed residencies in Oklahoma public schools, delighting children and adults alike with his lively, creative storytelling abilities. He has also taught Folklore and fables for the Great Expectation Institute at Northeastern State University in Tahlequah Oklahoma. Al has traveled from Massachusetts to New Orleans, sharing the folklore of Africa, and African Americans, in his one-man performance, *Fabulous Fibs, fables and Folklore...*

Currently, Bostick is listed with the Oklahoma Arts Council, and The Arts Council of Oklahoma City, as a teaching artist and mentor. Al Bostick, as performer and visionary, has been an inspiration to audiences and a mentor to many emerging young artists in theater and storytelling.

**Cynthia Laws CALLOWAY** is a storyteller, extraordinaire. She specializes in telling stories of women from the Bible and African American *sheroes* and heroes. She is a lover of Old Negro Spirituals so you may hear her break into a song as she tells her stories.

She has a Bachelor's in Psychology and English Literature from The Colorado College, and a Master's in Education, Guidance and Counseling from University of Central Florida. She recently completed a Master's in Arts and Culture from Phillip Theological Seminary.

She is a retired Oklahoma Licensed Professional Counseling (LPC) and worked with trauma and families involved in the Murrah Building bombing, May 3 tornado and the 9-11 terrorist attack. She now enjoys coaching and counseling individuals to overcome barriers to achievements their goals.

She is married to Roosevelt Calloway and has three daughters, three sons-in-laws, 10 grandchildren and three great grandchildren. She and Roosevelt are both from Florida and hope to retire back there some day.

**Rosemary CZARSKI**- *"Soft, gentle and easy on the spirit, her stories take us to other places and times and bring smiles to the face."* Rosemary Czarski has lived in Jones Oklahoma for most of her storytelling career. In 1982, she embarked on her journey as a public storyteller by telling and reading stories to preschool children as a children's librarian. As she learned more about storytelling at conferences and workshops, Rosemary became avid to tell stories to other age groups. Over the years, she has shared her passion for the storytelling art with her husband, Richard, their two children, and five grandchildren. When Territory Tellers formally incorporated in 1985, she became a member. She was active on the

Territory Tellers Board of Directors serving first as secretary-treasurer, then secretary, and for many years as liaison director.

Rosemary's unstinting support of the art as a library administrator, storytelling leader and arts advocate was recognized in 2005 with the National Storytelling Network "ORACLE" Award for Leadership and Service in the South Central Region at the NSN conference in 2005. This recognition underscored her invaluable service in hosting storytelling, acting as liaison among diverse community groups to promote storytelling, and her support and encouragement of new storytellers.

Rosemary has told stories at workshops, open microphone opportunities, in the library and classroom, and at formal and informal concerts all over the state. She started out focusing on folk and fairy tales and then moved into personal stories.

In the late 1990's, Rosemary was part of a small group of tellers gathered informally at local libraries to share stories and information. This launched the next phase of her storytelling adventures: offering workshops on basic storytelling for teens and adults and organizing half and full day mini-conference type workshops where many storytellers could share information. The Art of Storytelling, an ongoing series of workshops she started then is still occurring in 2014. Rosemary has been a member of, and coordinator of events, for the WayWord Tellers since 1999.

When talking about the basics, she advocates that the teller keep the process and story simple, to learn from others and to practice constantly.

**Michael CORLEY** -- Michael Corley is a Master Magician and Storyteller who has made a career of entertaining children for over twenty years. His magic show is a combination of high energy stunts, dancing rope, floating dollars and mysterious levitations!

*"Several years ago I finished a performance in Luther, Oklahoma. I was in full Native American dress as part of the program, including loincloth, beaver skin breastplate and a breastplate and a coyote headdress. My character, 'Waziatah, great north wind', stepped into the changing room and out came Michael Corley, mild mannered business man with glasses, suit and a tie. While carrying my speaker equipment out a young child approached me. He has broken away from the line back to class and said he enjoyed Waziatah so much he wanted to give him a quarter. He asked if I could give it to him.*

*It took me a half-second to realize he didn't recognize me! I told him Waziatah would want him to give the quarter to charity and that I would pass along the message to him.*

*As the boy walked away, I reflected my boyhood
dream had just come true. I was Superman! This
boy had seen me, no mask, just a costume and didn't
recognized the boring normal me just because I was
wearing a suit and glasses! That child couldn't know
what a thrill that was for me, but it's a memory I will
always cherish as a storyteller."*

After graduating with a degree in Radio-Television-
Film from the University of Texas, Michael moved
to Oklahoma where he worked in radio broadcast for
seven years. Currently, he is a professional magician
specializing in children entertainment including
school, libraries and birthday parties!

Michael uses his talents as a storyteller and magician
to make kids smile traveling to all over Oklahoma.
He explodes on the stage in costume, voices, and a
rowdy verve that engages audiences instantly. [89] He
has been a popular, and regular, feature of children's
programs for summer and beyond.[90] He was
recognized as a clear community celebrity when he
participated in an event to highlight the value of

---

[89] See a video at "Storyteller Michael Sings…"
http://www.youtube.com/watch?v=Hsr8pzD6RQY
[90] "Storyteller Plans Visit to Seven in Pioneer Library
System." Oklahoman. (June 27, 2004)pg.5EAST.

reading in 2004.[91]

He also works on television and radio as an actor and voice-over for numerous projects including Two Movie Guys, Broadway Weight Loss Clinic and Edmond Hyundai. He's premiered in the movie "Army of Frankensteins" as President Lincoln's Secretary. He writes articles on children entertainment for My Kids Adventures. He is also a cartoonist with two weekly publications including "Vox in a Box". He has videos that give the flavor of his magic performances.[92]

Michael lives in Edmond with his wife, Jennifer and daughter, Isabel. [93]

**Kyle DAHLEM** – As an educator for 42 years, Kyle Dahlem has long believed that stories are the essence of life, culture and belief. With that philosophy, she has used stories from many places and times to increase understanding in her students of all ages. From China to Africa to the United States and

---

[91] "Area Celebrities to Display Skills at Library Event." Oklahoman, (April 17, 2004)pg. 8NORTH.
[92] Magic: A Banana cut by magic! ; Dancing Rope magic! Michael Summons the Ghost Casper!
[93] See his page at Vox
http://michaelcorley.voxboxcomics.com/about/; permission to reprint this information from Michael Corley, 2014.

countries in between, these places provide the wisdom and fun of ageless tales that Kyle tells.[94] She has been a featured performer at various festivals and concerts.

She shares her story sharing inspirations: "The biggest influence on my ability to tell was my mother, Louise Roberts, and I have no doubt that she, likewise, was influenced by hers. As the Mother of five rambunctious children, she could weave a story or a story song in a moment to hold us spellbound or to lull us to sleep.

Mother also told me that as a student at Oklahoma College for Women (now USAO) how much she admired the performances of Ta Ata when Ta Ata returned to her alma mater. From 4-H Timely Topic competitions in elementary school, I developed a love of public speaking (weird, huh?)."

A child of a Methodist parsonage she experienced a lot of western Oklahoma in her children in Lawton, Apache, Mountain View Cheyenne, Wakita. "It was not unusual, to hear the stories of my Native American friends — even to attend Pow Wows with them — thus my love of the Native American

---

[94] Kyle Dalhem, Biography, Territory Tellers website. Used by permission.

stories."

"In my first year (1967) of teaching, I discovered the power of storytelling in teaching! My challenge, as the freshman English teacher to over 140 students, was how to make learning grammar interesting and effective. Quite by accident one day, I told the story of the apostrophe with the multiple personality disorder! They laughed but they remembered its many uses.

Through the many years of teaching in Oklahoma, (in Fairview, Geary, Seiling and Moore) I found storytelling to be the best way for me to teach and for students to learn. Introducing units, elucidating challenging ideas, making the boring interesting or just entertaining students, I loved the ways students responded to storytelling in the classroom. Teaching was more fun for me as well. If one wants to be a storyteller, one must first be a good listener."

**Jim ETTER -** Jim Marion Etter is a retired reporter for *The Oklahoman* who for years roamed Oklahoma and neighboring areas to research and write about out-of-the-way places. His work helped set the stage for an appreciation and interest in Oklahoma's rich, and sometimes weird, history as a source for stories to tell.

His books include "WHAT A DIRTY SHAME! 101 Unforgettable Place Names of Oklahoma"; "Ghost-Town Tales of Oklahoma -- Unforgettable Stories of Nearly Forgotten Places"; "Thunder in the Heartland," Second Edition; "The Grains of Time"; "Oktaha, A Track in the Sand"; and "Between Me & You & the Gatepost – Rural Expressions of Oklahoma."

He is among the authors in the anthologies of "New Trails – 23 Original Stories of the West"; "Black Hats"; "Daughters of the Land"; "Western Horse Tales"; and "The Salt of the Earth." He also has written for such magazines as *Persimmon Hill, American Cowboy, Western Horseman, True West, Desert Exposure, Route 66, Oklahoma Today* and *ByLine.*

Etter, of Bethany, is a native of the small Muskogee County town of Oktaha. He has also lived and worked as a journalist in Laredo, Texas, and served as a military writer and translator in Latin America. He also spent several months in New Mexico, researching and writing about Billy the Kid and Pancho Villa.

He presently works as a teacher's assistant for Putnam City Schools.[95]

**Jeanette HARJO** – "*Smooth, capable, and deep; this storyteller pulls stories from deep places and weaves them together into interesting and unexpected patterns.*" You may find Jeanette Harjo wading in Blue River, delivering a new foal, skeet shooting or conducting classes at a local university, but wherever she's found you can bet she is gathering, writing, listening to or sharing stories. Storytelling activities and workshop presentations range from trail rides to national and state level conferences and festivals. She admits she can't live on concrete and has grown to accept she's just a "country girl with attitude". If you ask her when she first started telling stories she might reply it may have been while at the kitchen table with Grandma and the button jar or when she started repeating

---

[95] Permission to reproduce this information from Jim Etter, 2013.

colorful language overheard at the local sale barn. She is currently working on a book titled, <u>Horses, Handshakes, and Hand Grenades,</u> and her short story, <u>The Yeller Colt</u>, appeared in the Red Dirt Anthology.

She is the Past President of Territory Tellers, one of the original co-founders of the Spirit of Oklahoma Storytelling Festival, and former member of the Tejas Board of Directors.[96]

**William Phillip HARJO**--*The wisdom of multiple experiences and the ability to see the humor and the light and the insight in the lives he shares so warmly.*

Phillip Harjo was born in Shawnee, Oklahoma and spent his childhood in Seminole County. He attended Maud High School and continued his education at East Central University where he completed his bachelor's degree in health and physical education and graduate courses in counseling. Later he returned and acquired certification in all areas of science with exception of botany. Educating and helping others has been passion in all areas of Harjo's life.

A person who stepped up to challenges without hesitation Phillip Harjo has served as a mayor of a small community, as president of the Seminole County OEA, chairman of the tribal election board, chairman of the honor council, state liaison for

---

[96] Permission to reproduce this information from J. Harjo, 2013.

Territory Tellers, member of the board of directors for Tejas and has changed more flat tires for strangers than he can count. Harjo was eager to help when the call came out to organize and seek funding for the 1st Spirit of Oklahoma Storytelling Festival.

He spent 30 years in public education and held sixteen areas of certification. As a coach, teacher, and alternative education counselor, Harjo used stories to teach and touch lives of students. He says, "Stories are the common denominator among all of us." Harjo occasionally took breaks from public education to work for the Seminole Nation of Oklahoma. In 1976, as Director of Native American Programs he wrote the grant to establish the early childhood program which is still active and successful today.

While employed by the Indian Health Service Advisory Board, Harjo served as Mental Health Educator for Oklahoma and Kansas. After retiring from education, he accepted an invitation from Chief Enoch Kelly Haney to serve as his Chief of Staff. Jokingly Harjo claims working in tribal government is a story within itself.

Harjo is a retired Major of the U.S. Army Reserve and veteran of Desert Storm. Harjo received many awards and accolades while serving his country. Early in his military career he received special recognition for being the outstanding leader among his officer candidate class. Later he received a medal for heroism. Harjo served in the Oklahoma National

Guard where he led a Scout platoon and was requested to serve as an instructor at Officer Candidate School. After transferring to the Army Reserve he was Headquarters Commander of the 95th MTC, a position he held when he volunteered for Desert Shield. While an officer and gentleman, Harjo often integrated storytelling into teaching situations as well as for motivation.

He always appreciated a good story but did not consider pursuing a different venue for his storytelling until his wife insisted he accompany her to a performance by Choctaw storyteller and author, Tim Tingle.

Harjo shares it was as though Tingle reached inside him and gently squeezed his heart. Tingle's story evoked emotions so strong and plucked a string of commonality running deep among all native people. Harjo realized he would no longer just share personal stories to motivate students nor humorous informal stories to entertain but instead take steps to research, locate, and preserve stories of his tribe. A grant from the National Park Service provided funding for Harjo, who owned a video production company, to produce a set of DVDs documenting and preserving the lifestyles and traditions of the Seminoles and allowed him the honor of interviewing tribal elders and former Chiefs.

Phillip Harjo has served as keynote speaker and motivational speaker for graduations, banquets, and seminars. His storytelling performances and activities have included Five Tribes Story Conference, Seminole Cultural Fair, Tejas Storytelling Festival, Spirit of Oklahoma Storytelling Festival, and numerous schools and organizations.

The stories Harjo specializes in include Native American stories, humorous stories, animal stories, and those of heroism, courage, and honor.

Although Harjo travels throughout Oklahoma and to neighboring states, he is currently renovating a 1949 barn and plans to be chief cook, bottle washer, stick horse rider and resident storyteller.

**Beverly Brown HART** – Has been a resident of Mayes County for 39 years. "I grew up near the Verdigris River in Nowata County; living in a house built before Oklahoma became a state." She attended a one room schoolhouse for a couple of years.

"My parents have been deceased almost 40 years. I began writing memories as I feared "we" would forget the stories with the passing years. I listened as my father, who was born in Indian Territory, would tell an occasional story. Mother, while more reluctant to share, has proved to be the inspiration for some of the stories. These stories....some being compiled over nearly 40 years are among the stories I tell.

Having researched family history "off and on" for decades, I knew the true stories about real people should not be lost. I like to quote Mark Twain, Abraham Lincoln, and Will Rogers as an "ice breaker" when I speak.

My husband of 47 years lost a battle with cancer during the Great Blizzard of 2009; passing on Christmas Eve. I have two grown sons and grandchildren.

I owned and operated a tax preparation business for 20+ years before semi retiring. I served as substitute teacher at junior and senior high schools for 7 years. I have scaled back and now work from home doing a "comfortable" number of tax returns and bookkeeping. I continue as an enrolled agent dba Stone Cottage Business Svcs.

I volunteer at Church teaching an Adult Sunday School men/women class. The last year, I have served a Facilitator for organizing Day and Overnight trips for our Senior Group. The last trip was to view the Christmas Lights at Honor Heights Park in Muskogee. You got to love these people. One dear lady octogenarian managed to lock herself in the bathroom at the restaurant where we shared the evening meal. She managed to lock herself in the

"MEN'S BATHROOM".   After we got back on the bus, she came to me and said "Beverly I am really sorry I locked myself in the men's bathroom.  Things like that just happen to me." Like I say, you just have to love these people.  And I do.

I enjoy telling stories to various groups; usually community including schools, ladies groups etc.

Year 2013 brought a Blessing to my life.  My first book was published just before Thanksgiving.  It is available in hard copy and e-book.  Intended as a "family history book", it has been well received.  I am humbled.  It is entitled "Some of us were Patriots ~ Some of us were Prodigals"[97]

This picture was taken during a recent Church Trip. We traveled to eat at an establishment which was site of the filming of "Where the Red Fern Grows".

**Will HILL – MAHENWAHDOSE --** Will is a full-blood traditional Muscogean Indian, whose traditional name is Kabitcha Feke Sego.[98] Hill, who is of the House of Kings and the House of Warriors, was raised in the traditional arts of Native Storytelling, speaking his own native language, as well as the language of many other tribes. He is a graduate of the College of Santa Fe, and has received his acting training from well-known actors such as

---

[97] Hart. *Some of Us Were Patriots ~ Some of Us Were Prodigals*. August House, 2013.
[98] Permission to reprint this biography granted by Mr. Hill, February 2014.

William Shatner, Jane Alexander, the late Charlton Heston, Richard Thomas, and many others and was voted "Favorite Native American Performer in the State of Oklahoma in 1998". [99]

He has won numerous awards, including being the recipient of the Moscelyn Larkin Cultural Achievement Award in 2004 from the Greater Tulsa Indian Affairs Commission.[100] He is not only a performer, but a storyteller by destiny and is the greatest living Native American raconteur.

Mahenwahdose, a Muscogean word meaning "TRUE NATIVE AMERICAN THEATER," is a Native American Indian performance company founded in 1992 by Will Hill of the Muscogee Nation and Winona Henderson of the Cherokee Nation, and features the multi-talented performer, Will Hill.

Mahenwahdose/Will Hill brought national archival recognition to the State of Oklahoma and the Muscogee-Creek Nation by being the first American Indian to perform at the National Museum of the American Indian, Smithsonian Institute, Washington D.C. in July 2004, prior to its opening, and was chosen by the State of Oklahoma and Disney to represent Oklahoma's Centennial at EPCOT in Orlando, Florida in November 2007 with 31 performances.

---

[99] "Indian Actors Spin Tales". Oklahoman (April 21, 2002)3-A.

He has performed in over 3,000 venues and just recently had a national release of a song in which he provided the flute playing, voice over and co-composed entitled "The Trail of Tears" which can be heard on the "Song of America" album, produced by Grammy award winner David Macias and Ed Peterson. The album was nominated for a Grammy in 2008.

In March 2009, Will was recognized by the American Indian Resource Center as one of Native America's outstanding playwright's, having written numerous plays that have been performed at the Tulsa Performing Arts Center. The comedy "A Song of Winter," highlights "Christmas in Indian Country," and has been performed the last four years during the season of the popping trees, and the scary comedy "The Fearless Honkah Hunters," about the experiences of Native American Ghost Hunters premiered in October 2009 during the season of the big chestnut and was presented again in 2010 and 2011.

In addition to being the co-founder of Mahenwahdose, Will served on the Board of the American Indian Theater Company and the Greater Tulsa Indian Affairs Commission.[101] He is presently a Board Member of the American Indian Resource Center of the Tulsa City-County Library. His storytelling presentations include drum, flute,

---

[101] Judy Gibbs Robinson. "Tulsa Theater Company to Spoof Explorer's Arrival in New World." Oklahoman (Oct. 13, 2006)18A

language, song, comedy, and audience participation. When you hear his voice, you are also hearing the voices of ancestors of long ago.

**Marilyn A. HUDSON** – Hudson began telling stories while she worked in various school systems across the state (Enid, Oklahoma City, and Norman). Blending her degrees in history and library with her love of stories she shapes a variety of tales and has shared stories in several states. As a librarian in public and higher education libraries she was able to introduce students and adults to storytelling.

She has participated in many events across the state: the Oklahoma City Zoo, the OKC Art's Festival, Ponca City Heritage Days, Lawton Community

Theater[102], Encyclo-media (workshops and noon stories), Wintertales Olio[103], Wintertales Workshop[104], Enid Main Street First Friday Event, Oklahoma Celtic and Scottish Clans Festival[105], Spirit of Oklahoma Storytelling Festival, [106]Oklahoma City Storytelling Festival Olio, numerous churches, library systems, school districts, festivals and private events. She served several terms on the Board of Directors of the Territory Tellers, was editor for 'The Tattler", and contributed an original story to the storytelling sampler CD, *"Autumn Leaves and Stories Everywhere"* (Territory Tellers, 2002).

She traveled for over ten years each summer sharing stories in state libraries for their summer reading emphasis using dramatically presented stories,

---

[102] Kirsten Pupk. "Tradition's keepers headline show to benefit theater." Lawton Constitution (June 21, 2001)4B.
[103] "Oklahoma Olio", Winter Tales, Stage Center, February 6, 2004. Other performers were: Bonnie Smith (Prague), Gordon Green (Oklahoma City), and Teresa Black (Oklahoma City).
[104] Picture and bio appeared in the festival brochure of 2002; John Brandenburg. "Wintertales", Oklahoman (Feb.1, 2002). Article lists event and featured tellers but does not list others presenters.
[105] Picture and bio appeared in the festival brochure of 2003."Scottish Festival Planned", Oklahoman (March 11, 2002)9. Article records date and Edmond location but does not list all events.
[106] "In the End All You Are Is Your Story", Oklahoma Olio, flyer, Oklahoma City Storytelling Festival, September 10, 2011. Other tellers for this event were Pat Kardaleff (Lawton), Chester Weems (Yukon), Darla L'Allier (MC), and Greg Rogers (Warr Acres).

*"Storytivities"* (ca. 1999, a storytelling-learning module, often with costumes that shared life and tales of other places or times) and by adding participation story skits to 'activate' the storytelling experience.[107]

She served as facilitator to several storytelling groups (Norman, Oklahoma City and online) and producer of several Tellabration events (Oklahoma City, Norman and Bethany) and storytelling programs in Oklahoma City, Norman, and Bethany.

In 2003, she developed a storytelling persona, "The Ghost Teller." Specializing in tales of ghosts, hauntings, legends and her own imagination she has presented workshops, concerts and made personal appearances at paranormal and story conferences. She performed for several years at the Overholser Mansion as the "Ghost Teller" for the "Scary Tales and Twilight Tours."[108]

In 2005, she was awarded for *"Outstanding Contributions to Storytelling in Oklahoma"* by The Friends of the Metropolitan Library, Territory Tellers and the WayWord Tellers for *'instructing*

---

[107] "Activate" was used by Hudson to respond to the learning differences of children and help make classic library story times fun through movement, dance, hand and finger plays, and similar activities. In 2001, she wrote a story time manual for the Metropolitan Library System building on those key element to enrich library programs for preschoolers-elementary age children.

[108] "Norman Author, Storyteller to Perform", Norman Transcript (Oct. 23, 2011).

*others in the art and craft of storytelling'.*[109]

She wrote the narrative frame for the story program, *Casting Strong Shadows* and traveled with "Stories2Go" for several years. In 2012 she was a "Celebrity Reader" for the 2011 NSK Neustadt Prize for Children's Literature at the University of Oklahoma.[110]

She cites as some of her influences all the wonderful performers who visited the schools and libraries where she worked. Supporters on her story journey included Jonette Ellis, Jan Fischer, Lynda West, Jeannie Johnson, Letty Watt, Lois Hartman, Rosemary Czarski and Elizabeth Ellis.

For many years her logo was a spiral, because "stories journey inward to be experienced and then spiral outward to be shared. I still think that is an apt description of the process of storytelling and listening."

**Barbara Wright JONES-** *"Deep, moving, heartfelt stories of people, their challenges and their hopes."* Barbara Wright Jones is an educator, storyteller, award winning published author, and workshop speaker. In 2013, she won the American Christian Writers Award for her novel, *Anna's Song*.

---

[109] "Certificate of Appreciation", Elizabeth Parker, President of Territory Tellers, November 17, 2005.
[110] "Oregon Author Honored with Neustadt Award." Norman Transcript ( Sept.30, 2011).

She has a B. S. in Education, and an MA in Theology and Ministries from Bethany Nazarene College [now SNU] and is an ordained elder in the Church of the Nazarene. She and her husband were career missionaries and she has served as an instructor in the Ministerial Course of Study in their denomination for many years.

Barbara begin telling stories of the Bible to children when she was only a teenager. She learned that even the most difficult children were drawn to stories and she fell in love with both teaching and storytelling.

Her experiences and stories include multi-cultural depth reflecting her years working in South America. She authored a book of finger puppet plays and curriculum books for Spanish language teachers. Her stories are creative, personal, often with interactive activities, and listeners of all ages enjoy her presentations.

Although loving tales of folklore, myth and fiction, a love for Bible storytelling grew and became especially helpful when she lived abroad. There, she found that her gift for storytelling opened the understanding of Scripture to those of different cultures.

She has performed story programs in many venues including churches, libraries, festivals, schools, and teacher workshops. She has been a Territory Tellers board member, past president of PAWS writers association, a member of Respect Diversity

Foundations Speaker's Bureau, and the Oklahoma Performers and Presenters.

Presently she lives in Oklahoma City, Oklahoma with her husband, Kenneth. They have three married children and five grandchildren.

**Pat KARDOLEFF** – Oklahoma born, Pat has been an elementary teacher and has actively used storytelling in the classroom. She has shared tales at festivals, community venues libraries and schools across the state.[111]

**Steve KARDOLEFF** - A storyteller with Macedonian roots, living in Lawton, Oklahoma. He is the past executive director of the National Storytelling Network. In addition to performances, he has frequently led workshops on storytelling creation and interpretation. One of his stories, *Nasreddin Odjah's Clothes*, was featured in a book, "Treasures from Europe: stories and classroom activities." His impact on the story community is far reaching and often expresses itself in surprising ways.[112] As the organization moved into producing the Spirit of Oklahoma Storytelling Festival his experience and insight was invaluable in creating a quality festival.

---

[111] Kirsten Pupk. "Tradition's keepers headline show to benefit theater." Lawton Constitution (June 21, 2001)4B.
[112] Steven provided some crucial help to one of the authors of **Inviting the Wolf in: Thinking about the Difficult Story** By Loren Niemi, Elizabeth Ellis (2001) pg. 173f.

**Valerie KIMBLE** - Valerie Kimble has told stories in schools, libraries, churches, treatment centers, and performing art centers to audiences of all ages.

"If you sit still a minute, I will tell you a story," she says. She is well-known in Southern Oklahoma for storytelling performances in Ardmore and surrounding communities. She has performed in Oklahoma City at Olio's and Tellebration's hosted by the Territory Tellers, the statewide storytelling organization.  As part of a storytelling delegation to Egypt in November 2009, Valerie told stories at the Library of Alexandria.

In 1992, along with Stephanie Billioux, Janine Evard, and Scott and Tina Saner, she co-founded the Word Weavers, a storytelling guild for the greater Ardmore area.  Valerie served twice on the Board of Directors of Territory Tellers of Oklahoma, where she chaired the Publicity Committee for the Spirit of Oklahoma Storytelling Festival, and currently serves on the Board of the Tejas Storytelling Association, headquartered in Denton, Texas.  She is a member of Territory Tellers, Tejas and the National Storytelling Network.

Employed by the Pioneer Library System as a children's librarian and storyteller, she lives in Norman with her husband Jim.

Sometimes with puppets and props, or more often with her voice alone, Valerie creates the world of the story for her listeners.  Regardless of location--in their seats or up on stage with her--Valerie makes the audience an active partner in the performance.[113]

**Jahruba LAMBETH** – Although his family has been in Oklahoma since the Landrun, Lambeth terms himself a 20th century *Griot* (an African storyteller) who shared his cultural history and traditions through songs, drumming and stories handed down by his ancestors. A winning way with audiences his talent delighted audiences of every age. Smoothly moving from jazz improvisation to heart drumming that brought to life giant elephants and creeping lions.

Jahruba has been performing professionally for over 35 years. His approach is to use authentic artifacts, folk-tales, songs and instruments to teach young and old about Africa and the African American experience. He selects stories that encourage young people to think for themselves -- such as the story of the greedy hunter of Ibo village who found out the hard way about the power of greed, or Fulumbo of the Fulanis, the handicapped boy who saved his village from Zulu raiders with the magical rhythm of peace. There are stories of Ananzi the spider, always up to tricks, and many more.

In addition to a BA in African Studies from San Francisco University, Jahruba has studied with master drummers and street musicians from around the world.[114]

---

[113] Valerie Kimble, Norman, OK, February 2, 2013. Permission to reproduce.

[114] "Meet the Storyteller: Juhruba Lambeth", Oklahoma Tellers, at http://oklahomatellers.blogspot.com/2008/06/meet-

**Molly LEMMONS** – Award winning author, storytelling and workshop leader, Molly has been telling stories all of her life. After years of working for Mustang Public Schools, she retired and devoted fulltime to writing, telling stories, and teaching workshops.

Molly's stories have been published in *Chicken Soup for The Mother's Soul*, *Christian Woman*, *Christian Chronicle*, *Christian Journal*, *and Ideals Magazine*. She was also published in *Chicken Soup for the Kids' Soul 2,* and *Heavenly Patchwork*. Her stories have also appeared online in online publications as well as newspapers in Arkansas, Texas, and Oklahoma.

Molly adapts her stories to suit any age group and setting. She has performed in concerts at Winter Tales, Spirit of Oklahoma Storytelling and numerous venues across the state and in the region. Her workshop on "How to Write Life's Memories" blended her skills as a storyteller to make classes come alive.

She is also the author of several books. Former governor Frank Keating noted, "Molly looks at life through a prism of faith, hope and love." Her works include *Kind of Heart, The Passing of Paradise, Seize the Flashbacks!* and *Pure as the Driven Snow*

---

storyteller-jaruba-lambeth.html; "Juhruba, Inc." at http://www.jahruba.com/ accessed February 4, 2014; author interview with Lambeth 2012.

A former first-runner up for the title of Ms. Senior Oklahoma, Molly belongs to The Age of Elegance Club, which as former contestants and winners, performs all over Oklahoma City several times a month for Senior Residence Centers.

Molly is ongoing advocate for storytelling. "Anyone interested in storytelling will find many rewards and benefits as you revive memories in minds that have long forgotten their roots, relive historical moments, make up lively and exciting tales to a general audience." She also entertains children with stories that all ages can enjoy. "You will find," she notes, "that entertaining people and making them smile, or touching them with a thought or bringing a tear of gratitude, or happiness or remembrance, is its own reward."

Molly is an alumna of Oklahoma Christian College and spent most of her life around the Oklahoma City area. Her memories of life the way it was in the capitol city, her children, grandchildren and her cats inspire many of her tales. She currently resides in Mustang with her husband of her over fifty years, Freddy.[115]

**Stella LONG** - *"She takes you by the hand on a journey into the soul of people, into the heart of stories, and you are compelled to go because of her*

---

[115] Brochure, "Miss Molly Lou Belle with Tales to Tell" and website 'Miss Molly Lou Belle" at www.mollyloubelle.com. Used with permission.

*loving attention to those people."*

Stella Long grew up in Choctaw Nation in eastern Oklahoma. She lived and enjoyed the marvelous world of the animals and birds and learned their behavior as a child. Times were difficult for the family and at the age ten, she was sent to Goodland Indian Boarding School to further her education. Unfortunately, in her senior year she became ill and was hospitalized for several years with tuberculosis. During that time, she was taught by a special education teacher and she finally had her diploma. She had wished to be a registered nurse, but at the time of her discharge the doctor informed her she should never consider being a nurse, and suggested a desk job. She was advised to stay home for six months before doing anything.

After that time, Stella enrolled in continuing education classes at Central State University, two technical schools, and a business college. She became a medical transcriber for a pathologist. Later, she was employed in the Office of Business Affairs at Rose State College. While there, she did her first classroom storytelling.

Following her retirement at Rose State College, she joined the Toast Master's organization to help her become and effective public speaker. Tim Tingle guided her further into the world of storytelling when he taught at the College of Santa Fe. She recently published a short story for children, "Sarah's Music" and now working on a novel based on her life story.

She also has short stories she plans to publish following the novel.

She tells humorous and traditional stories. Her life stories goes into an intensely personal level and she has no regrets of living the emotional hardship that have brought forth wisdom and prospective from living those years. She shares the healing stories to support people to find their own way to heal physically, emotionally, and spiritually.

Stella was asked by members of the Choctaw Alliance to establish a yearly Inter Tribal Storytelling for the public. The next one will be held during the summer. This will be announced.

Listing of places stories told: Universities, public schools and libraries. The Smithsonian National Museum of the American Indians in Washington D.C.; Oklahoma State Capitol with Choctaw Nation; Montgomery College, Germantown MD.; Oklahoma Correctional Facility for Women; Under privilege Boy's Home, held at Eagle Ridge Institute; Nursing Home for Alzheimer's patients; American Indian Tribal facilities; The Goodland Indian Boarding School, where she went to school, now known as "Goodland Christian Boys Home."

Her Motto: Friendship, kindness, and laughter are good medicine!

For the Oklahoma Centennial, Stella was part of a special costumed program, *History from the Heart*.

The troupe comprised of women from The Territory Tellers, included Liz Parker, Bonnie Smith, Molly Lemmons, Stella Long, Barbara Jones, Susie Beasley, Jeanette Harjo, and Kathryn Thurman.

They combined to portray women from their own families that helped build this great state of Oklahoma. These women may not be found in the history books, but they all reflect the great Oklahoma spirit.

**Maureen MAGOVERN** – A certified teacher (B.A. Ohio State University) she taught elementary children in the regular classroom as well as in special arts, Spanish language, visual arts and gifted programs.

As an employee of the Pioneer Library System MaGovern worked with children, teens and adults and used her skills to enliven presentations and classes. She attended Storytelling and Drama Workshops at the Oklahoma Fall Arts Institute and became an active member of Territory Tellers and the Norman Storytellers. She co-produced the Norman 2002 Tellabration event and provided storytelling programs in all of the nine branch libraries and for special events including: "Mid-Autumn Moon Festival: Vietnamese Stories and Fun", "Bears, Beasties and Books", "Winter Holidays: Stories of Light", and "Benjamin Franklin Through the Eyes of Deborah, His Wife."[116] Her

---

[116] "Library to host Tellabration event." Norman Transcript ( Nov. 15, 2002)A9. Other artists performing for the event

other performance experiences included telling at the Oklahoma City Zoo and at the Omniplex (2002). She was featured performer for the Moore Public Library annual Holiday Gala (2002).

**Nancy MATTHEWS**—*"With stories that dare and challenge us to do something out of the ordinary and look for the mysterious in common places."*

**Barbara MCBRIDE-SMITH** - Barbara McBride-Smith grew up in Texas, was educated in Massachusetts, discovered the ways of the world on the Jersey shore, and finally settled down in Oklahoma. She has been a school librarian for 44 years and a seminary professor for more than 20 years. As a performing storyteller, she has entertained audiences across the U.S. and is frequently featured at the National Storytelling Festival in Jonesborough, Tennessee. She is a member of the National Storytelling Circle of Excellence and a recipient of the John Henry Faulk Award for Outstanding Contributions to Storytelling. [117]

**Sam MCMICHAEL** – *"Gentle, funny, humble Sam--just Sam. His stories leave you feeling young again and glad you were in his audience. One can never listen to him "too many times," and no one ever*

---

included: Michael Corley, Marilyn A. Hudson, Jahruba Lambeth, Lynn Moroney.
[117]

(http://www.barbaramcbridesmith.com/barbara_mcbride_smit h_003.htm) *leaves without feeling like someone just threw a bushel of "warm fuzzies" right straight into their heart."*

Take a boy out of the rural environs of Oklahoma, send him to a classroom, stir in some teaching, some thinking and a lot of living and set to simmer. The result is Sam McMichael whose ability to take the simple to new and dazzling heights is only challenged by his ability to connect with minds and hearts with audiences of every age. He has actively promoted a love of storytelling and the value of the art to address various personal and social issues.[118]

**Shaun PERKINS** - Shaun Perkins grew up in the small northeastern Oklahoma town of Locust Grove. She wrote stories and poems from the time she could write and loved typing them on a pale blue Brother typewriter. She also wrote poetry that she folded and hid beneath the tiles on her house.

After earning a bachelor's degree in English from Oklahoma State University, Perkins went on to Kansas State University and took graduate courses in creative writing and then to Northeastern State University, where she enrolled in the education program to become a secondary English teacher. As a teacher at Bartlesville High School, Coffeyville Community College, Pryor High School, and Oaks

---

[118] Kirsten Pupk. "Tradition's keepers headline show to benefit theater." Lawton Constitution (June 21, 2001)4B.

Mission High School, Perkins enjoyed teaching and nourishing a love of stories in her students.

She currently teaches part-time for both Rogers State University and Bacone College. Teaching and performing have been part of her life for many years, but her decision to become a professional storyteller was activated by her involvement starting in 2002 with a personal growth community in Missouri called Diana's Grove.

At Diana's Grove, Perkins encountered a supportive community of people in love and captivated by the arts of storytelling, poetry, dancing, drumming, and more. Her skills as a storyteller and poet were honed and developed there. This experience of community compelled her to begin Mayes County Storytellers, co-founded with her sister Roxann Perkins. The organization put on Tellabrations for several years and participated in the Territory Tellers' annual storytelling festival.

Perkins has presented workshops in storytelling at many festivals and conferences, including the Spirit of Oklahoma Storytelling Festival, Story Circle Conference, Popular Culture Conference, National Storytelling Network Annual Conference, National Association of Poetry Therapy Annual Conference, Kansas Authors Conference, Oklahoma City Storytelling Festival, WinterTales, and more.

The stories that Perkins specializes in include mythic stories about women, Oklahoma wildflower stories, scary stories, humorous folktales, and personal stories about growing up female in rural Oklahoma.

In 2011, Perkins created the *Rural Oklahoma Museum of Poetry*, in rural Locust Grove. The museum has had hundreds of visitors since it opened and has been the focus of a story on NPR's State of the *Re:Union* show. The museum received the Douglas Noverr Grant for museums from the Popular Culture Society in 2014 and continues to grow its collection and schedule a variety of events that bring poetry (and storytelling) to people from all walks of life.

As a poet, Perkins frequently brings poetry into her storytelling, combining the rhythms of poetry with the organic form of storytelling to make a unique experience, a journey in words.

As Ray Bradbury once said, "Let the things that you love be the things that you do and the things that you do be the things that you love." Perkins lives according to this motto, and while it hasn't been financially easy as a poet and storyteller, she would not change a thing about her experience and continued involvement in these worlds.

**Greg ROGERS** – A member of the Choctaw Nation of Oklahoma, Greg is a writer, storyteller, workshop presenter, and oral historian. He has performed in front of hundreds of audiences, sharing stories designed to both entertain and educate. Greg's storytelling began professionally, years ago, under the mentorship of noted Choctaw storyteller and author Tim Tingle. From there, the writing progressed naturally under the same guidance. While completing a degree in Native American Studies at the University of Oklahoma, with recognizable names such as Geary Hobson, Clara Sue Kidwell, Barbara Hobson, Jerry Bread, Rilla Askew, N. Scott Momaday, and Gus Palmer, Jr. he continued to explore and express himself.

In July of 2009, Rodgers was honored with an invitation to participate as a workshop presenter for the Young Native Writers Essay Contest winners at the Smithsonian Institute's National Museum of the American Indian. Later, the Smithsonian Institute again called and asked Greg to participate in their outreach program. He was invited to Casper, Wyoming where he performed in area schools and The Trail Center. He received great reviews and was added to the program's list as an official Smithsonian Associate He has also guest-lectured and performed at such universities as Rice, Southeastern Oklahoma State University, Oklahoma University, Southwestern Oklahoma State University, Wayne State University in Nebraska, and Southern Nazarene University in Bethany, Oklahoma.

Greg's short story, "Harriet's Burden," is included in the 2006 Nov/Dec special Native American issue of *Storytelling Magazine*, the membership publication of the National Storytelling Network. This story is the first in a series of short stories based on family remembrances. An accomplished Native American flute player, Rodgers has performed and presented workshops at schools, libraries, and tribal events throughout Oklahoma. He has performed stories in front of diverse audiences, including the *Choctaw Nation Storytelling Festival*, held annually in McAlester, Oklahoma, and the 2006 *Okla Chahta Gathering* in Bakersfield, California. He is a descendant of Reverend Israel Folsom, a co-author of the first Choctaw dictionary and prominent Choctaw leader in both Mississippi and Oklahoma during the 1800's.

In June of 2009, Rodgers was a featured regional teller at the *Spirit of Oklahoma Storytelling Festival*. In March of 2008, he performed during the Native American Concert at the Texas Storytelling Festival in Denton, TX.

In between the writing, telling, and collecting of stories, Greg had served as board member for both the Oklahoma Choctaw Tribal Alliance and Territory Tellers, the Oklahoma state storytelling organization. He has also been a regional vice-president for the Folsom Family Association.

Greg's storytelling repertory includes both traditional and contemporary Choctaw stories, family stories, and travel stories from the year he spent in Prague, Czech Republic teaching English as a Second Language.

Over the summer of 2006, Rodgers completed a storytelling mentorship under the direction of professional Choctaw storyteller and author Tim Tingle, sponsored by the University of Oklahoma. In addition, he has studied the craft of storytelling with nationally respected and acclaimed Appalachian master storyteller Elizabeth Ellis. Greg's performances are a public demonstration of his true passion, the collection and respectful preservation of his people's memories----the foundation of the Choctaw oral narrative.

**Sally RIFFEY** – Sally is a native of Oklahoma City and feels that her roots go deep into Oklahoma's red clay. Her stories have been called *Stories from the Heart.*

"I have been told that I was born telling stories," Sally Riffey noted. "Well maybe not but it is true, I do love to tell stories! It is my passion! Before my children were born I started collecting wonderful books that I wanted to read to them. I became so familiar with the stories I could tell them anytime, anywhere which has come in handy many times! When my children were in school their teachers would ask me to watch their class when they had special meetings or appointments. What a great time to share my stories! Since that time I have become a "Professional Storyteller" and grateful for the opportunity to share my love and passion for Storytelling!"

All Storytellers are unique. If you put six Storytellers together on a stage and gave them the same story to tell, each story would be told differently!"

As a Storyteller, Sally enjoys telling folktales, original stories and stories of the season, but retains a deep passion for Biblical stories. She has been a participant in the annual Easter drama The Great Plains Passion Play.

"My major influence in telling stories comes from the love and encouragement of my family and friends and, without a doubt, the Lord Himself! My favorite stories are those shared at Biblical sites in the Holy Land."

Additionally, Sally does Biblical portrayals of Mary Magdalene and Mary the Mother of Jesus in Biblical costume as a solo drama presentation. A highlight of Sally's storytelling career was the recent opportunity to tell Biblical stories at several sites in Jerusalem and at the Sea of Galilee.

Sally has taken her stories behind prison walls to state and federal prisons. She has been a featured teller at many Tellabration and Oklahoma Olio concerts. She has also told stories at WinterTales, the Oklahoma City Arts Festival, for the opening of the Oklahoma Trails at the Oklahoma City Zoo. She frequently tells stories for civic organizations, women's ministry groups, churches, schools, professional business groups, as well as Easter and Christmas presentations and programs.

Sally is a member of Territory Tellers. She is also a past board member of Deaconess Hospital Health Venture Corporation.

"The best advice I can give to someone who wants to be a Storyteller is to tell stories from your heart. Stories filled with your own passion. Many of us have shared stories that have been told from generation to generation...which is the true spirit of Storytelling!"

**Bonnie SMITH** – *"Her heart and spirit shine through her stories, stories that often feature unique corners of Oklahoma's past."* Bonnie was a middle-school teacher of English and Literature in Prague, Oklahoma. She was an avid advocate of storytelling in the classroom and used storytelling to engage the students in learning. She organized the Statehood Day Celebrations in her region and was instrumental in obtaining a Citation from the Oklahoma House of Representatives and a Proclamation from the Governor of Oklahoma proclaiming November 12-19, 2003 as Storytelling Tellabration Week in Oklahoma. Her performance venues have included festivals (in Oklahoma and beyond), arts celebrations, schools, libraries and community events. As President of the Territory Tellers she worked tirelessly to promote and expand the reach and horizon of storytelling in Oklahoma.

**Kathryn THURMAN** – *"Contemporary Native American Storyteller and Flutist"* Kathryn Thurman is a professional Musician and Storyteller who uses her unique musical background to create entertaining stories that can be enhanced with different types of music. Audiences may see such instruments as the psaltery, slide whistle, finger cymbals, spoons, kazoos, and percussion frogs. She has spent the last twenty years performing in schools, libraries, museums, Girl Scout camps, civic groups and community events. Each program is crafted with an element of fellowship, friendship, and fun, perfect for any type of audience.

A published Author and Book Reviewer, she travels to diverse locations to perform for audiences of all ages, such as preschool children who love animal stories, Book Clubs looking for a book review, Seniors who enjoy family stories, school students learning about the Land Run, and Scouts who love Ghost Stories at the Campfire.

With a background involving over fifty theatrical and musical productions, Kathryn brings the spontaneity of the theater into her performances. When possible, she adds audience participation and interaction by teaching a song or dance movement, clapping a lively rhythm or rap rhyme.

Kathryn's background includes a (Muskogee) Creek Great-Grandmother who shared her heritage through stories, and began Kathryn's journey that has led her to becoming an accomplished Native American flute musician and teacher.

**Chester WEEMS** – *"Stories from this man are like a fond memory of a walk down a sunny street, they bring a smile and add a bounce to the step. Not to be missed."*

Chester Weems is an Oklahoma storyteller and a retired educator. He grew up in northwest Oklahoma in Dewey County. Graduating from Seiling High School in 1961 he went on to college at Southwestern and then to the University of Oklahoma. He taught geography at Louisiana Tech University, a year at Southwestern in Education, and worked in Mustang Schools and Mid-Del Schools for a total of 36 years in teaching and administration, and after retirement another 6 years as an educational consultant.[119] Along the way he developed skills in photography and storytelling. He is known as both a storyteller, and a photographer of tellers. Here are his thoughts.

"I have always loved stories, all kinds of stories, but real ones over fiction. I remember, as a kid out on the farm, Mom would tell about growing up in OKC, going to movies, and seeing professional wrestlers. She made it so exciting I thought she was personal friends with most of them. She would read stories to my brother and me, and I would read library books from school, plus the stories and *Aesop's Fables* from the old 1918 set of *The Book of Knowledge* we had at home. We did not have TV, and our battery operated radio only worked periodically. About ½ mile east of our house lived a farmer, Art Abbott, a

---

[119] Amy Greene. "Grant Links Area Seniors to Computers." Oklahoman (February 12, 1999)85.

friend of my granddad. I still remember a magic afternoon sitting on a bench in his cool milk house listening to him tell stories of people and places.

It was not until years later, probably in my 50's, that I actually was exposed to organized storytelling. I started attending "Wintertales" in OKC and found out about an Oklahoma organization called "Territory Tellers." After several years I finally found the nerve to stand up and tell a short story in a workshop, and over the years telling has become easier and easier.[120]

Sometimes I think I am getting better at telling; then I hear a good teller and have to reassess. But, mainly, I am finding my voice where I can share and enjoy presenting. I have been fortunate to have attended a couple of Elizabeth Ellis weekend workshops, as well as a number of short workshops by national tellers at regional festivals. I am in awe of people who can put words together that create pictures or stir emotions.

Most of the stories I do have some basis in an actual family event, either my own or an event someone has shared and allowed me to retell. When I see real people and real places in my head, it makes it easier for me to remember the story to tell, though it never comes out the same. I do admit my stories got better when I didn't always let too much truth get in the way. Few things exceed the pleasure of seeing an

[120] Ann DeFrange. "Storytelling Celebrations Observed This Month." Oklahoman (Nov.9, 2004) 1 South.

audience nod their heads, or smile, or even laugh at your words.

Along this path I also have very much enjoyed photographing tellers doing their thing and have a good collection of photographs of Oklahoma tellers and many of visiting tellers to Oklahoma festivals. Many I share with the tellers, not for profit, but for the pleasure it gives me, and hopefully them.

I encourage others to collect their own stories for their families. I tend to be guided by two sayings I have heard: "When an old person dies, a story is lost," and "In the end, all you are is your story."

**Dwe WILLIAMS** – *"Dynamic, visionary, and compelling; her creative talent and managerial drive are a source of inspiration. It does not matter if she is telling stories or creating wonderful plays to celebrate Black History Month with the talented cast of Rhythmically Speaking, she is dynamo of creative energy."*

**Laurette WILLIS** - For over twenty-five years, Laurette Willis has been invited to entertain and speak to groups. Including touring U.S. Armed Forces in Asia with the U.S.O. and visiting with over 500,000 students in schools & universities since 1993. An award-winning actor and playwright, she studied Theater Arts at New York University, and Artist on the Touring and Teaching Rosters of the Oklahoma Arts Council she epitomizes the many art forms that use and build on the storytelling art and the strong relationship of theatrics with traditional storytelling.

A popular Keynote Speaker, Laurette ignites her messages with a unique blend of heartfelt encouragement, touching personal stories and side-splitting humor. Laurette's comedic edge was sharpened Off-Broadway in the 1980's as an improvisational comedienne, where she earned the nickname: "The Woman of 101 Voices!"

As a playwright and Director of DoveTale Productions, Laurette is known for bringing history-to-life in over 20 original one-woman shows and ensemble productions for a variety of community & historical organizations since the early 1990s. Her one-woman show, "Great Women of the Frontier" was presented at the National Governors' Conference and aboard the Delta Queen Riverboat for the Smithsonian Institute. From 2007 - 2011, she directed and performed in the summer outdoor drama she wrote for the Cherokee Heritage Center and National Museum, Under the Cherokee Moon, near her adopted hometown of Tahlequah, OK, capital of the Cherokee Nation.

The Creator of the **PowerMoves Kids Program** - the first Character Education & Fitness Program for the classroom (used in public schools, private schools and home schools throughout the U.S. and Canada) - "Winning the War Against Childhood Obesity -- with CHARACTER!"

An author with Harvest House Publishers, Laurette has written several books and has produced a dozen Fitness DVDs and two television fitness shows currently reaching over 100 million globally.

Laurette's most requested Storytelling program, **"Historical Hysterics"** is geared to an age group (pre-K through adult). This energetic, interactive storytelling session, sometimes called a cartoon for the mind, includes "The Snake Story" (with its important "Be Drug Free" message it is popular during Red Ribbon Week). As a master ventriloquist she brings an added dimension to her work and younger audiences also meet a chatty turtle who lives in a Cherokee basket – and won't come out. Additional programs such as **Great Women of the Frontier** combine elements of "Historical Hysterics" to an older audience making it educational and entertaining.

Older students help Laurette re-enact Sequoyah's 1820 Syllabary experiment, where he proved to his people that the Syllabary (Cherokee Alphabet) could help the Cherokees advance by sharing their wisdom via "talking leaves" (books and the written Cherokee language). Realizing that Sequoyah (George Guess) grew up without his father's influence, that he suffered a physical handicap and was often ridiculed by his peers, students learn about overcoming obstacles, the high cost of leadership and the importance of following one's dream.

Laurette and her husband Paul live on a 40-acre ranch in the beautiful Ozark foothills of northeastern Oklahoma.[121]

---

[121] "Ponca Theater Awaits Frontier Woman Show." Oklahoman (August 19,1993)10; "Great Women of the Bible" at ." Oklahoman/Norman Edition. (Feb.13, 2004)6.

# CHAPTER 8
# STORYTELLING
# PIONEERS

The following people are identified as pioneers due their significant role in promoting the art form, supporting its development, and leading fellow story artists to new levels of achievement. The list is not, cannot be, complete at this point. These, however, are the individual's whose status and obvious leadership ranks them as pioneers of the story art in modern Oklahoma.

**Teresa BLACK -** In the Middle Ages, entertainers with music and story would roam the courts and countryside. These storytellers, often called troubadours or a minstrels, would share history, romance and satire in equal measure and were welcomed by all. That legacy is one that performers such as Black carry on into the twenty-first

century.[122]

"I was born in the first half of the last century, in
1948.  My story songs reach across three centuries,
starting with tales of my 1800's relatives who made
the 1889 Land Run and lived in Oklahoma Territory.
I relive a bit of the Old West as a historic reenactor
and bring the 1800's alive in my songs and stories."
In truth, Black was one of a large group of women
who blazed a trail for participation in Civil War
historical reenactments in the 1990's. [123]

I'm a cast member of the Pawnee Bill Wild West
Show.  Some see me in my calico dress, singing an
old folk song at a historic fort and say I look like a
ghost from the past.  I sing at the Oklahoma History
Center several times a year.

My life has lots of adventures as I travel to sing and
tell stories.  I've been in parades, in wagon trains
attacked by bandits, stage coach robberies and
rescued by Pawnee Bill and his cowboys. I've sung
at art festivals and story-telling events, sometimes

---

[122] Bernice McShane. "Oklahoma History Something to Sing
About." Oklahoman (March 15, 1992)76.
[123] "Union Soldiers Repel Attacks", Oklahoman (July 19,
1993)104. This article includes a photo and the label "An
assistant U.S. attorney during the week…";  Audrey DeFrank.
"Journey to an Era." Oklahoman (July 16, 1995)69. David
Zizzo. "Women Re-Enactors Spark Own Civil War."
Oklahoman (May 11, 1997)237 and same date "Women Spark
Reenactment Battlefield (pg.1).

enlisting children and senior citizens to play along on the tambourine or washboard. I've sung at the Alamo historic site, and at battlegrounds and forts from Tennessee to Kansas.

I was born in Oklahoma City. My father told me stories of his grandfather who made the Land Run and founded some of the most infamous saloons in the new Territory. One was the Black and Rogers Saloon where Oklahoma City's city hall was once located on the floor above. My father told of Gov. "Alfalfa Bill" Murray, the bridge war with Texas, of outlaws and shootings of fame.

I have a CD, the Oklahoma Waltz, which includes songs and stories of Oklahoma history. My song "The Peddlers Books" was used in a video by Faultless Starch. Several of my songs have been honored in various contests. My songs are available on CDbaby.com.

I am married to Ed Bradway and now live in Clayton, Oklahoma, in the Kiamichi Mountains, with Fritz the dog. I have a few published mystery short stories. My photos and writings appear in local newspapers. I volunteer at the Clayton Senior Center. In 2013, I retired after almost 38 years as a federal prosecutor. I attended public schools in Oklahoma City and am an OU grad – but married to an OSU alum."

**Connie FISHER** – *"Rare and special, his vision of life and his memories combine to create one of kind delights."*

"In March of 1991, I was teaching in Rockwall, Texas when a storyteller, Dale Bulla, was brought to the school. I visited with him about 'Storytelling' and as a result I joined the Dallas Area Storytelling Guild. Since then, I have had membership in the Tulsey Town Yarnspinners, The Tejas Storytelling Association, the Territory Tellers, the Tallgrass Tellers, the River and Prairie Storyweavers (RAPS) and of course, NSN, the National Storytelling Network."

Fisher has been a popular performer for a wide variety of events. Using a casual yet often subtly dramatic style he has been a popular storyteller for special events, community events, and storytelling celebrations.[124]
As a storyteller, he tells from all venues with stories for children, adults and care facilities. "I feature some Scot and Irish and personal narrative stories. For over twenty years I was with the Artists in the School Program of Tulsa, Oklahoma."

He has been a featured teller for the Bartlesville, Oklahoma 'Sunfest', the Territory Tellers "Spirit of Oklahoma Festival" and Tallgrass Tellers "Tellabration." "Five times I have been an invited teller for the "Texas Storytelling Festival" in Denton,

---

[124] "Storytelling Event to Include Yukon." Oklahoman (Nov. 14,1997)2.

Texas." In 2009, he was a recipient of the NSN 'ORACLE' Award for Service and Leadership.

"As everyone is a storyteller," Fisher asserts, "I enjoy helping new working tellers find their voice."

**John HINKLE** - Librarians, a wit has noted, seldom retire. They simply go out of circulation. Not true for John Hinkle. This library professional who traveled to every library in the state when he was a consultant at the Oklahoma Department of Libraries and performed as storyteller and puppeteer in every Oklahoma county but three, continued to entertain after his retirement. His history with the Oklahoma Arts Council stretches back 25 years as puppeteer, Artist-in-Residence, musician and storyteller. Although retired, he remained active and developed a program portraying 'Alfalfa Bill' at state locations in 2007.[125]

"People always tell me what a good storyteller I am," Hinkle said. "And I always have the same reply for them. If you chose a story that's been around for a hundred to a thousand years, it should be good for another 45

---

[125] "Alfalfa Bill at Ada Library". Ada News (April 17,2007) accessioned at http://theadanews.com/local/x212588095/John-Hinkle-to-portray-Alfalfa-Bill-at-Ada-library/print); see also "Storyteller Creates Cast of Characters" at http://newsok.com/storyteller-creates-cast-of-characters/article/2556971; also the OLA Legends page at

minutes."[126]

In 2007, he noted his soon retirement from traveling with puppets. "Next year will be 50 years of puppets, so I'm going to hang up touring with all the stages and equipment. With the Oklahoma Centennial upon us I thought a rousing puppet melodrama would be good to close with in 2007, so I'm doing *How Straight Shooter Saved Sweet Sal, and the Oklahoma Seal from the Vilest Villain in the Whole Wild West.*"[127]

**Lynn MORONEY** -   This artist has been a creative and innovative leader in the state since the early 1870's. As lecturer to school groups visiting the Kirkpatrick Planetarium at the Oklahoma Science and Arts Foundation in Oklahoma City she merged story and art. In her lectures she began blending interesting background information and stories into the science based presentations to engender interest in her youthful audiences. At the time she was pursuing a degree in elementary education and became the right person in the right place to begin the development of her own unique creative style.

In 1973, as arts coordinator for the local arts council, she developed a multi-sensory touring exhibit designed to

---

[126] "Uncle Remus Due at Library." Grove Observer. Friday, June 23, 2006 accessed at http://thegroveobserver.blogspot.com/2006/06/uncle-remus-due-at-library.html.

[127] Ibid.

showcase the art in everyday objects. Desiring to teach that not all art had to hang on a wall the exhibit, known as "The Art Field" and "Common Sense" was six feet of items to see, touch and hear.

In 1989, after several years as a storyteller, she expanded her creative world through a partnership with well-known Oklahoma resident and fellow Chickasha Tribe member, Te Ata. Adapting the other woman's near signature tale, Moroney published *Baby Rattlesnake* (1989), followed by *Elinda Who Danced in the Sky* (1990), *Moontellers* (1995) and *The Boy Who Loved Bears* (1994). Baby Rattlesnake became a popular children's picture book and helped spread awareness of Native American folklore, Oklahoma storytelling and the two storytellers themselves.

With a background in the Sciences and Arts, teaching and lecturing in Astronomy, the "Mother of Science," she teamed up with fellow Oklahoma story artist, Fran Stallings to present "Earth and Sky Stories." This pioneering program capitalized on the special expertise of the two: Moroney as astronomical lecturer and Stallings with a PhD in Biology. The two have crisscrossed the land with this program.

Moroney's career on the Oklahoma storytelling stage, and the broader arts community, has been marked by richly creative leadership and activity.

**Sky SHIVERS** – *An audience member described the performances of this cowboy influenced teller as "hot coffee on a cold morning; that is how his stories* *feel." Another enjoyed the 'come right here and sit for a spell' warmth that bewitched and entertained the audience.*

Humorist and storyteller, Sky Shivers, was inspired in the reality of being a "chronically unemployed cowboy." With a family, he realized the cowboy world was a "great life but a lousy living." As a result, he heard about some programs going into local schools and libraries. Thinking about his options, he realized he had gained a lot of information over the years about the pioneer, farming, and cowboy life. He hauled out an antique trunk and gathered some of the "old things" decorating the house. With the trunk, the artifacts and the stories he had heard from old farmers and cowboys, he launched into the living history project of the early 1990's to share "the life of a homestead kid."

Claiming no skills as a storyteller, his easy charm, authentic and natural sense of humor, carried the day. He said he had no plot, no script and no two shows were alike. He intuitively knew he had to adapt to the needs and interests of the current audience. At the peak of his career sharing with the trunk he was doing about 300 shows a year in Oklahoma, Texas and southern Colorado.

Shivers credits his major influence as his family. He described them as having traditional habits and values. His grandmother was part Cherokee and Black Dutch. She left a lasting impression because she believed a man should have a pretty wife to come home to and as a result she was known for her love of bright red shoes, purses, and a lipstick she would apply to ensure a freshly "pretty face." Whenever the family gathered there would be stories and memories shared.

At the local feed store filled with aromas and what he calls "antique sweat" he would hear the stories of old men gathered around the classic stove. Going hunting with family, he would hear the tales of other hunts and as he did the work of a cowboy, he absorbed the stories. Sometimes he even overheard things that later saved his life. Shivers shared a tale of stopping in a little diner one day when he overheard two older men talking in the booth behind him. One of the men was sharing how he had been hunting a cow when it burst out of the brush "blowing snot and fire." Running as fast as he could the old man said he had "donated his hat" to stop the animal's charge. Shivers wondered what in the world the man might mean but it was soon forgotten.

It was far from his memory years later as he was working a rodeo for a Dude Ranch. The stands were crowded with people who had come from New York for the exhibition of steer wrestling, bull riding and barrel racing. One rider was trying to ride and was bouncing around the arena hung up on a bull. He had raced out to successfully help the rider and distract the bull. As the animal turned and sighted the lanky Shivers the phrase of that old man in the diner came to clear life. The bull focused on him and turned toward him "blowing snot and fire." Racing toward the side of the arena, he glimpsed his wife Debora and daughters looking pale and stricken. He could feel the hot breath of the beast on his back and "leaped 25,000 feet in the air" to jump over that barrier and find safety on the other side of the wall.

Over the years Shivers has worked with many organizations and groups promoting the arts and history. What he has learned from those experiences is the importance of learning history and being proud of the diversity and unique nature of Oklahoma's past. Working with children and youth, he is quick to encourage them to learn their family history. "I tell them to be specific. Ask them questions and get them remembering and talking," he noted. "What your first car? Where did you go on your first date?" In response to one adult, who spoke to him after a class he taught noting she had no good stories to share. Her family had a significant tragedy in one generation she could not share and did not wish to share. "Emphasize the positive where you can and then skip a generation if you have to, but give them that sense of family."

The ultimate goal of Sky Shivers is to become "one of those cantankerous old men" he had met so often in those feed stores. They taught him that you have to "live some life before you got something to do." He has something to do now and he does it very well.

**Rodger HARRIS -** *"Blending together folk songs,*

*folk tales and skillful delivery this performer can charm any audience with a lively and authentic touch."* Professionally Roger Harris has had a diverse yet interconnected range of experiences. He has served as the Oral Historian, Director of the Outreach Section of the Research Division, Director of the *Oklahoma Folklife Center* of the Oklahoma Historical Society, and creator-editor of "Oklahoma Folks," an online journal of Oklahoma folk life.

Harris was born in Duncan (Oklahoma) and raised in Marlow (Oklahoman). He earned his B.S. in Business from Oklahoma State University (1968). Later, he added an M.A. in History from University of Central Oklahoma (1982).

He has published widely over subjects dear to his personal and professional interests: "Notes On Dulcimer Making" Bois d'Arc Press 1978 ;"Whatever Happened to 3D Danny? The First 25 Years of Television in Central Oklahoma", *Chronicles of Oklahoma.* 1992; "The Bean Story, *An Anthology of Stories From the Tejas Storytelling Festival*", August House Publications, 1995. "Opus 5281: The Story of the Kilgen Theater Organ at WKY Radio, the Civic Center Auditorium, and the State Museum of History", *The Chronicles of Oklahoma.* 1999. Wars of the Confederacy, Wars with the Indians, and Wars with the "Fiddle and Bow": The Life of Henry C. Gilliland and "It Was In This Way": The Influence of Oral Tradition on Life And Literature of Oklahomans, *Oklahoma Folks* (the online journal of the Oklahoma Folklife Center).

For some 25 years he had performed with the *Falderal String Band* performing music in the traditions of the Southwest. [128] His experiences as a storytelling performer include: Wintertales, (Oklahoma City); The Tejas Storytelling Festival, (Denton, Texas); The National Storytelling Association, (Jonesboro, Tennessee); The Port Fairy Folk Festival, (Port Fairy, Victoria, AU); The Illawara Folk Festival, (Jamboroo, New South Wales, AU) Ozark Folk Center, (Mt. View, Arkansas), Tulsey Town Tellers Festival, (Tulsa,

---

[128] See the band's web page at: <falderal@cox.net>

Oklahoma). [129]

***Fran STALLINGS*** - *"Sure, deep, and enriching are how to describe Fran's telling as she blends from a rich resource of talent and experience to create tales that delight."*

Fran Stallings has been based in Bartlesville since 1975 and a Professional teller since 1982. In her professional story career she has been as a professional touring teller; an Artist in Residence with the Oklahoma Arts Council 1985-2001; an Artist in the Schools with Tulsa Arts & Humanities 1988-present.

Her range of storytelling expertise include traditional, original, ecological/science, history; and Japanese folktales.

Her experience in storytelling has been statewide, nationwide and extensive overseas trips. After years in the professional storytelling field, she easily notes that "It just keeps getting more fun!" She has conducted numerous workshops and inspires others to pursue the art form. "The best way to refine your skills, "she advices, "is to tell to a variety of audiences and learn from their reactions."

From 1995 to 2008, Fran managed the American tours of traditional Japanese storyteller/educator

---

[129] Contact information: Oklahoma Historical Society, 2100 N. Lincoln, Oklahoma City, OK 73105 Contact: <rharris@ok-history.mus.ok.us> (405) 522-5207.

Hiroko Fujita. Together they received NSN's International StoryBridge Award. Fran and Lynn Moroney (Earth & Sky Storytellers) offer unique two-day "Celebrate Science" programs which provide teachers with in-service training during the regular school day while students experience story concerts and special activities.

Her peers had recognized her for her work as an artist and advocate. Fran received the 2007 Service/Leadership award from the National Storytelling Network for her work as NSN's Oklahoma State Liaison and for her contributions to state and regional storytelling organizations. She received the 2009 John Henry Faulk Award from the Tejas Storytelling Association for her contributions to the art of storytelling in the Southwest. One example of this is her leadership in co-founding the Tallgrass Tellers, a storytelling group in Bartlesville, OK. In addition, Fran has produced numerous recordings and publications.[130]

**Wilna TIPPS** – When she retired in 1986 Tipps was working with the Norman Public Library as a children's librarian. She had worked in Norman in 1957 and again in 1971.

She had over three decades of experience in libraries. For the retirement reception members of Territory Tellers shared stories in her honor: John Hinkle,

---

[130] "Fran Stallings" © Storyteller Fran Stallings.1406 Macklyn Lane, Bartlesville OK 74006-5419; 918-333-7390 [Used by Permission]

Roger and Marie Harris, Pat Nelson, and Chris Hull.[131]

She had also worked in the Metropolitan Library System's branch in Del City and shared stories in numerous locations. [132] It is believed she retired back to her early home residence in Carter County and died there in 1998.

**David TITUS** - David Titus, author and professional storyteller, has been entertaining children and adults in libraries, schools, churches and at conferences and festivals since 1968. He travels extensively, consulting, conducting workshops and residencies, instructing adults in storytelling, and collecting stories and string figures. He has entertained audiences across six continents from the frozen Arctic to the Sahara. With a piece of string and a thread of a story he captures his audience, young and old. Needless to say, he is having a lot of fun doing it.

Collecting string tricks from Tibetan refugees in Nepal, Pakistani refugees in Cairo, or a traveler in the Seoul airport; he then shares them in other parts of the world. This Master Storyteller spent five weeks in Nepal in 1999 renewing acquaintances he made in 1997. He traveled to very remote regions to help at leprosy hospitals, teaching the patients to make

---

[131] "Moore Librarian to Be Honored". Oklahoman (Dec.1, 1986)57.
[132] 'Closed' Sign Doesn't Affect Use of Library." Oklahoman (Aug.18, 1966)45.

string figures as physical therapy. He went to Nepal again in 2006.

Spending August and September 2000 in Mongolia, Titus took 20,000 strings to give the new organization "String Ministries" the acid test. The nomadic Mongolian people loved the diversion and activity these games provided. Eagle TV, the local Christian station had him on two live programs, translated all three of his videos for airing, and shot almost two hours of short testimonies and stories to be inserted in future broadcasting. He returned to Mongolia in August 2005.

Since 2001, Titus has gone to England to work in schools, prisons and churches and took two trips to Mexico to share his talents with string and collect information on the use of string figures in their culture. He has made three trips to Eastern Europe spending up to six weeks in Latvia, Lithuania Estonia, Poland and Finland working in churches, schools, prisons, a refugee camp and orphanages. In 2002, Titus took the first of two trips to South Africa and a mission trip to Belize. He went to South Africa and Namibia and made two trips to a Refugee camp for Liberian refugees in Ghana, West Africa. Venezuela was worked in there somewhere before relations with that country became so tense.

Taking his guide and translator from the States he made a trip to Papua New Guinea in October 2006. He stayed in the mountains with the tribal chief and his 5 wives. A wife cost 30 pigs there, so the chief was a rich man. He went to Australia on that trip also. He also returned to Poland in 2007. He spent a month living with a Palestinian family in the West Bank in 2008 and then went to Bolivia before that country was closed to travel. He seems to be just ahead of trouble. November and December 2008 will see him in Pakistan living with a family there and visiting surrounding villages with 3,000 strings.

In between his overseas travel, Dave works with schools in the United States spending a full day or two at a school turning kids on to the world of string. What great brain gym activities these are.

David Titus is now the author of "Native American String Figures", "African String Figures" and "Native Alaskan String Figures." These oversize soft cover books have pictures and written directions for making a number of figures that Dave has collected on his travels.

The video "String Magic From Around The World" has been a favorite with many schools, libraries and families since it came out in 1997. "This video shows more than 50 string figures, gives directions for over 20, and includes a practice string. It provides live-action demonstrations and storytelling with string figures," School Library Journal, October 1997.

Titus' first in the series of Christian string videos is "String Fun with the Parables." Video Librarian gave it 3 stars out of 4 in the July/August review and School Library Journal said in June 1999, "This engaging introduction to the Old and New Testament Parables will appeal to Christian schools and churches and to public libraries where its cross generation appeal will be a plus."

Titus has a video that explains the mission and goals of String Ministries, Inc. This 31-minute video titled "Sharing with String through String Ministries," gives practical examples of how string figures can be used as a tool for mission trips, youth groups, retreats etc. Directions for each of the figures are included in the video. His forth video, "Exciting Christian String Figure," was released in 2009. It is also designed to be used with children and youth groups, youth working with summer camps and VBS, and individuals going on mission trips. All of Dave's video works are being produced in DVD format to bring them into the new century.

These DVD's and books, plus audiotapes, strings and other string related products are available for purchase at www.StringFigureStore.com. Titus estimates that Goodwill Industries, Inc., who has the contract to provide the labor to produce the colorful knotless strings that he provides, will produce over 100,000 this year.

Titus has been a librarian in Ohio, Michigan, Honduras-Central America and Oklahoma and was also with the Oklahoma State Department of Education as a consultant to library and media programs. He has been active in storytelling and was president of Territory Tellers, the Statewide

Storytelling guild.

**Letty WATT** - *Once Upon a Time There Was a Young Girl Who Told a Story.* – "I must have told a duesy of a story when I was in 4<sup>th</sup> grade because I remember the kids laughing which prompted the teacher to call my mother in for a conference. "If Letty would just pay attention in class instead of dreaming up stories, she could be an A+ student." Then again it might have been in 2<sup>nd</sup> grade when I became a storyteller, because that was the year we moved into a duplex on A st S.E. In my upstairs bedroom I discovered that my slanted closet contained a painted picture of a raw and bloody bones skull complete with dripping blood red paint. I entertained the neighborhood kids many times from the confines of that tiny closet.

In reality, I began my career as a storyteller for the Miami Public Library when a new show called Sesame Street was taking over the minds and imaginations of children, and at the time, my young daughter would listen to stories nightly. I needed a gimmick or reason for parents to bring their children to the library instead of watching TV.

Luckily, a woman at the Oklahoma Department of Libraries named Mary Ann Wentroth willingly drove to Miami, Ok to teach a one-day class on storytelling. She was to return in two weeks, but no one else really wanted to be a storyteller. So it was six months later when she drove to Pryor, OK for a storytelling workshop that I had a chance to tell my first ever folktale. Mary Ann became a coach and mentor for me for the next few years.

By 1977, I was conducting storytelling workshops in Kansas, Colorado, Texas, and Oklahoma while learning to be a puppeteer and working full-time as an elementary librarian in Greensburg, KS. From 1975-1984, I conducted summer workshops at various colleges and universities on storytelling and puppetry. I helped to organize and tell in the first storytelling event in Oklahoma sponsored by the Tulsa public library in the early 80's featuring Doc McConnell and Laura Sims, and local talent. Storytelling was a movement nationwide thanks to the The National Storytelling Festival, Jimmie Neil Smith, and the Folktellers, Connie Regan and Barbara Freeman.

I worked as a librarian with the Norman Public Schools from 1978-96 during which time I co-authored two books on Learning Skills, storytelling being one of them. With the help of Lynn Moroney from the Arts Council of Oklahoma, and Roger and Marie Harris, Rosemary Czarski, and others we organized the Territory Tellers, early in the 1980's, holding regular meetings, conducting workshops around the state and telling stories on every stage we could find. I was the first President of Territory Tellers, and enjoyed every story we shared. By then Texas had an annual storytelling festival and Oklahoma began with a spring stage at the Arts Festival until moving to Winterfest.

Since moving away from our Oklahoma roots in 1996 my husband and I have found new friends and stories in Kansas.  As a middle school and then elementary classroom teacher I worked with students on storytelling and puppetry skills.  Several of my students have been selected as Storytelling Torchbearers for the state, one student, Renea Cikanek,  was selected for the National Youth Storytelling Olympics in Jonesburg, Tennessee, then a few years later two of my fifth graders, Liz Woody and Tori Humes were selected to tell in the first duet storytelling performance at the National Youth Storytelling Olympics.

Even though I am retired from public education, I still make time to tell stories for a variety of audiences; my puppets follow me and share the stage when possible.  When I'm not telling stories, I can be found writing stories on my blog, many of which find their way to the storytelling stage.  I am so proud to say I was a founding member of the Territory Tellers, and whenever possible I come back to my roots to hear a good story.[133] – Letty Watt (2013)

**Mary Ann WENTROTH**, *a Storytelling Mentor* – "Miss Wentroth was the Children's Services Consultant for the Oklahoma Department of Libraries when I got my first job as a Children's Librarian for the Chickasaw Regional Public Library

---

[133] If you'd like to read her stories please go to my blog "Literally Letty" at http://literallyletty.blogspot.com/ or if you are looking for a storyteller for a program contact her at letty.watt@cox.net

System in Ardmore, OK in 1977. [134] She planned wonderful trainings for all the children's librarians in the state, but the best one I ever attended was a storytelling intensive that lasted 3 or 4 days in the spring of 1978 or 1979.[135]

Miss Wentroth was able to bring Augusta Baker and Ellin Greene to Norman, OK to demonstrate storytelling. Both women had been librarians for the New York Public Library, which has a very strong tradition of providing storytelling programs to children of all ages. They had recently collaborated on a book, Storytelling: Art and Technique (1st edition, 1977—Note: This text is in its 4th edition, 2010 currently co-authored by Ellin Greene and Janice del Negro.). Ms. Greene had two compilations of folktales in print at the time, Clever Gretel and Midsummer Magic, as well. Children's librarians from public libraries all across Oklahoma attended. Held at the Continuing Education Center on the University of Oklahoma campus, it was a magical experience. Practical advice on conducting story times in libraries was provided, of course, but at the start of each day, one of the storytellers told stories until lunch. We laughed, we cried, we sat with open mouths as these master tellers performed. I know of two participants at that seminar who

---

[134] Wentroth was also Children's Services Coordinator for the Metropolitan Library System as noted in "Closed' Sign Doesn't Affect Use of Library.' Oklahoman (Aug.18,1966)45.
[135] Gail Mitchell. 'Library's Retiring Kid Consultant Says 'Children are Important People'. Oklahoman (Oct. 19, 1979)75.

became professional storytellers, Sue Ellen Stillwell (now of Fort Collins, Colorado) and myself.

I never heard Mary Ann Wentroth tell a story; but I consider her a great mentor for planning, organizing and facilitating that experience." —Valerie Kimball

# Closing Thoughts

This brief history has been able to merely skim the surface of all the information related to storytelling in modern Oklahoma. Just how it might march into the future may depend on how it is perceived by the public, how it responds to new cultural influences, and how it embraces its own integral diversity.

This work, along with the storytelling activities of so many gifted artisans, may help to raise awareness of the scope of modern storytelling. To provide some assistance in showing that storytelling is as foundational to adult life as to childhood. We are truly never too old for the magic of a story told well and with substance. In stories are found the perfect communication medium for they are equally capable of entertaining, instructing, stimulating thought, and sparking action.

As the rivers of culture, technology and creative invention all run together, storytelling will do as it has always done in balancing an ancient art form with an ever changing modern landscape. The symbiotic relationship with visual art, theater, music, and poetic forms is well recognized. In more recent times an acknowledgment of the potential for similar partnerships has emerged for authors and those in technological and alternative social and cultural fields (story slams, digital, LARP, Steampunk, etc.).

As storytelling enters the 21$^{st}$ century a question is posed as to its nature: is it jazz or ballet? Does storytelling have the vigorous and untamed improvisation of jazz music as its essence? Is storytelling the rigidly defined movements, approved postures and styles of ballet? Is storytelling, perhaps, more a magical middle group of creative exploration built on solid, and proven, traditional elements yet flexible enough to evolve?

One of the realities unearthed in this study was the multi-faceted nature of the people called storytellers. For the most part these creative individuals cannot be limited to a single expression of their vision or energy. They play musical instruments, they teach, they write books, they write and act in plays, they compose poems, they are political and social advocates. They do a host of other things revealing that to be a 'storyteller' means that narrow definitions and rigid limitations simply do not apply.

Down-home yarn spinners, gritty urban 'slammers', acrobatic-leaping-story-acting entertainers, music-story sharers, puppet accompanied performers, suave raconteurs, highly stylized story bearers, and casual person-down-the-street styles are all storytelling in modern Oklahoma.

The metaphor of a tapestry has often been used in reference to storytelling and it is fitting when discussing the reality in Oklahoma. The complex patterns, colors, symbols, and textures of a tapestry reflect the state of storytelling in Oklahoma.

As communities, schools, libraries and individuals write their own stories, other supporters, pioneers, innovators, and artisans will be uncovered. As they are brought to light, the understanding of relationships, influences, and benchmarks of achievement may all have to be shifted to accommodate those new facts and styles. That is an exciting potential.

Also, as the popular understanding of storytelling adapts to recognize the integral diversity and necessary fluidity of forms as part of the strength of the art form, it will become a vital force in society.

Story sharing, like music and art, is one of the few cross-generational forms of human artistic expressions. People never out-grow stories because stories grow with people. They keep pace with human activity, provide the light in the darkness of human pain, issue the motivating challenge to ignite action, and become the inner voice to spur us over forbidding obstacles of life or imagination.

One of the catch phrases of the storytelling community is ultimately very accurate. Everyone has a story in them. The history of storytelling in modern Oklahoma has essentially been one seeking to help people find and release that inner story.

In the process, the heritage of storytelling in Oklahoma will soar high into the skies stirring dreams and drawing the curious to discover new worlds through story.

*- Photo courtesy of Chester Weems*

*The audience enters the auditorium, they settle into their seats, low murmurs, a cough or two, all muffled by the heavy curtain of the stage.*

*In the wings, they wait, a little nervous, a little preoccupied, and anxious for the moment when the drapes pull back to reveal the empty stage.*

*The house lights dim, a rustle as the curtains open...the echo of footsteps heading to the spotlight ...*

*A hush falls, the audience eagerly leans forward as the story takes center stage.*

*What stories still wait to be shared?*

# List of Resources

For those of an academic bent, this list represents many of the common resources and writings related to the topic of this volume.

## Books
Colwell, Eileen. Storytelling. Bodley Head, 1983.

Livo, Norma J. and Sandra A. Rietz. Storytelling: Process and practice. Libraries Unlimited, 1986.

Pelloswski, Anne. The World of storytelling. H.W. Wilson, 1990.

Sawyer, Ruth. The Way of the Storyteller. Viking, 1942.

## Dissertations, Thesis, Etc.
Green, J. Rachel. Adult learning through storytelling: a study of learning strategies and philosophies." Dissertation thesis. Oklahoma State University, 2006.

Hannah, Leslie D. "We still tell stories: An examination of Cherokee oral literature." Dissertation thesis. University of Oklahoma, 2003.

## Archival /History Collections
O'Dell, Larry. Folk narrative and lore. Oklahoma encyclopedia at http://digital library.okstate.edu/encyclopedia/entries accessed May 25,2012.

Oklahoma Territory Tellers collection (1980-2005), Oklahoma Historical Society Research Division.

## Periodicals/Flyers
(listed in chronological order)
### General
"Sugar coating the realities of life." Oklahoman (September 28, 1917):6.

"Bullet stops storytelling policeman." Oklahoman (May

12, 1938):1.

Edyth T. Wallace. "Has story telling for small children become a lost art?" Oklahoman (January 14, 1943):6.

"Bedtime story revue dance dine." Advertisement. Oklahoman (May 16, 1951):61.

"Storyteller movie opens downtown." Oklahoman (February 26, 1953): 7.

"Anadarko Tribesman debunks Gallup claim to Indian capitol." Oklahoman (July 30, 1954):30.

"It's easy to make up tot's stories." Oklahoman (May 25, 1959):19.

"Christianity needs story-telling, Theologian says." Oklahoman (Nov. 23, 1973):94.

"Storytelling tips to be given: from a child's point of view." Oklahoman (January 22, 1976):24.

Sigrid Abbett. "Arts council coordinator sees art everywhere." Oklahoman (October 19, 1977):13.

Nancy Cook-Senn. "Art of Storytelling..." Oklahoman (February 4, 1977):24.

"Surprising twist in storytelling." Oklahoman (January 24, 1982): 193.

"Arts in residence program still growing." Oklahoman (April 28, 1985):113.

"WPA Listeners recorded stories of state's beginnings." Oklahoman (July 25, 1988)1.

Bernice Love. "Storytelling boosted as therapy." Oklahoman (January 19, 1988): 9.

"Fran Stallings." Territory Tattler (Winter 2007):3.

"Mrs. Overholser's Cookies." Preservation Oklahoma News (January 2007):7.

## Articles Indicating Misconception of Storytelling

"Author to stress the need to read." Oklahoman (March 2, 2001):5.

"Gifted Storyteller: 13-year-old Talks His Way from Britain to California." Los Angeles Times (4 Sept. 1972)a3.

## Ghost Stories/events

Ann deFrange. "Haunting stories to fill mansion." Oklahoman (October 25, 1992):237.

"Mansion scares up ghost stories." Oklahoman (October 17, 1993):93.

"Historic sites offering Halloween ghost tales." Oklahoman (October 19, 1997): 427.

"Historic sites reserved for ghost tale sessions." Oklahoman (October 13, 1998):38.

"Ghoulish tales to be told." Oklahoman (October 22, 1998):3.

Penny Owen. "Thrill, chill to tales at four legendary haunts." Oklahoman (October 28, 1999):15.

"Evening of storytelling." Oklahoman ( 2001)

"Tradition's keepers headline show to benefit theater." Lawton Constitution (June 21, 2001):48.

Klinka, Karen. "Haunting Options." Oklahoman (Oct. 23, 2003)17Edmond.

"Paracon Conference." Flyer. El Reno, Oklahoma. 2008. Author collection.

"Tour a haunted mansion." Overholser Mansion. Oct. 2010, at www.newsok.com.


## Libraries /Parks departments/Schools

"Hallwe'en Party." Norman Democrat (Oct. 1905).

"Story-telling Hour at Mission School." Oklahoma City Times (June 8, 1916)4.

"Many Children at Storytelling" Oklahoma City Times (October 14, 1916)1.

"300 Children." Oklahoman (August 29, 1915):5.

"Storytelling: Sulphur Circle League Plans." Oklahoma City Times (June19, 1917)7.

"Story Telling Hour." Oklahoman (August 3, 1917):57.

"Recreational center to be open Monday." Oklahoman (June 20, 1926):30.

"Children to crowd parks of city today." Oklahoman (May 31, 1939):5.

"Library starts plans to boost use of books." Oklahoman

(June 9, 1961): 19.

"Story time starts at city libraries." Oklahoman (February 9, 1965):26.

"Libraries slate storytelling." Oklahoman (January 25, 1966):43.

"Closed" sign doesn't affect use of library." Oklahoman (August 18, 1966): 45.

"Visit to county libraries a read adventure Saturday." Oklahoman (September 30, 1966):37.

"Libraries planning Christmas events." Oklahoman (December 6, 1968):69.

"Library moves in Edmond." Oklahoman (January 21, 1968):42.

"Crafts series posted." Oklahoman (October 17, 1969): 40.

"Libraries looking for storytellers." Oklahoman (August 19, 1977):22.

"Storyteller in schools." Oklahoman (October 30, 1977):169.

"Library hunting for storyteller who 'loves children and books'." Oklahoman (October 24, 1980):72.


### Story Groups/Groups Using Storytelling
"Mrs. Nannie Lee Frayser." Oklahoman (February 17, 1919):4.

"Temperance group will meet today." Oklahoman (March 8, 1940):5.

"School leaders to attend." Oklahoman (April 16, 1954):47.

"Club to meet on Wednesday." Oklahoman (March 28, 1956):8.

Ann Landers. "Storytelling tips are given." Oklahoman (November 2, 174):13.

"Storytelling Clinic Saturday." Oklahoman (February 15, 1980):83.


### Story Tellers Club and National Story Tellers League
"Twentieth century culture club." Oklahoman (April 9,

1913):4.

Oklahoman ( June 14, 1914): 11.

"Summer school at university well attended." Oklahoman (June 18, 1916):15.

"Story Tellers League." Oklahoman (May 20, 1917):35.

"The Story Tellers form club at university." Oklahoman (July 5, 1921):4.

"Story tellers map program." Oklahoman (February 1, 1929): 12.

## Storytelling Events/Events with storytelling

"Arts." Oklahoman (November 16, 1982): 103.

"What's going on." Oklahoman (February 7, 1982):174.

Metropolitan Library System. "Storytelling Workshop." Handout. National Cowboy Hall of Fame (April 28, 1990). Author's collection.

"Medieval Fair." Norman, Oklahoma. 1994.

"Scottish Heritage Festival." Edmond. 2003.

## Storytelling Festivals

"Bazaars, Shows, etc." Oklahoman (July 1, 1983): 84.

"Events schedule listed for first day of festival." Oklahoman (April 19, 1983):15.

"State lore to come alive in Tulsa Heritage Days." Oklahoman (June 4, 1984):19.

"Azalea festival set in Muskogee." Oklahoman (April 10, 1988):113.

"Frederick festival celebrates cotton." Oklahoman (September 29, 1990):9.

"Festival Schedule." Oklahoman (September 11, 1987):79.

"Red Earth activities to begin." Oklahoman (May 29, 1988):90.

Gregory Polk. "Tribal storytellers keep traditions alive." Oklahoman (June 8, 1996): 97.

"Rogers University plans film, storytelling events." Oklahoman (November 4, 1998):19.

"Spirit of Oklahoma Storytelling Festival." Territory Tattler (Winter 2007). Author collection.

"Spirit of Oklahoma Storytelling Festival." Territory

Tattler (Winter 2008):2. Author collection.

"Muskogee's Soulful Storytelling Evening", Oklahoma Music Hall of Fame, February 4, 2010.

"Movin' On---Stories of heart, stories of hope." Brochure. National Storytelling Conference, July 13-17, 2005. Oklahoma City. Author's collection.

### Storytellers
Vic Schoonover. "Altus head librarian pulls strings to tell stories." Oklahoman (February 5, 1984):9.

Mary Sue Price. "Storytellers to set young spines tingling." Oklahoman (October 25, 1985):16.

"Five schools get art programs." Oklahoman (September 30, 1985): 39. Fran Stallings.

"Moore Librarian to be honored." Oklahoman (December 1, 1986):57.

### Tellabration
"What's going on?" Oklahoman (November 22, 1991):47.

"Grownups gathering to tell tales tonight." Oklahoman (November 20, 1992):4.

"Storytellers to attend national event in city." Oklahoman (Nov, 20, 1992):118.

"Storytelling event Saturday." Oklahoman (November 17, 1993): 53.

"Stories to be told." Oklahoman, 1995. At Oklahoma City Community College.

"Storytelling event to include Yukon." Oklahoman (October 1997).

"Storytelling event Saturday." Oklahoman (November 17, 1999): 83.

"Spinning local yarns." Oklahoma Gazette (November 2000).

"What's going on." Oklahoman (November 17, 2001):38.

"Norman library to join in Tellabration!" Oklahoman (November 14, 2002):39-D.

"Library to host Tellabration event." Norman Transcript (November 15, 2002):A9.

"Calendar." Oklahoman (November 17, 2003): 2C.

"Tellabration." Territory Tattler (Winter 03-04):5.

Marilyn A. Hudson

"Tellabration." Territory Tattler. (November 9, 2004).
"Families." Oklahoman (November 14, 2005):2B.
"Weekend Look." Oklahoman (November 11, 2005):2D.
"Metro Library Events." Oklahoman (November 8, 2007): 3South.
"Tellabration". Flyer. 2007.

## Territory Tellers
"Oklahoma Territory Tellers dinner theater." Oklahoman (February 1, 1987):86.
"Storytellers band together." Oklahoman (Dec. 29, 1991):58.
John Greiner, Carmel Perez Snyder, Ryan McNeil. "States' Storytellers honored." Oklahoman. November 16, 2003):7A.
"Storytelling workshop set at library." Oklahoman (January 15, 2001):72.
"Oklahoma Olio." Flyer. Oklahoma Storytelling Festival (September 10, 2011). Author's collection.

## WinterTales (1982-2009)
"Professional storyteller to perform." Oklahoman (June 26, 1983):100. ; "Storytelling '83: Family Festival."
Chris Brawley. "You won't believe this one." Oklahoman (July 4, 1983):1.
"Festival to spotlight medieval storytelling." Oklahoman (January 3, 1985):18.
"Storytelling fete harks back to Medieval days." Oklahoman (February 1, 1985): 54.
"Winter tales to enliven winter arts." Oklahoman (December 28, 1985):15.
"Storytelling art form worth keeping." Oklahoman (January 26, 1986): 96.
"Seminars, concerts feature storytelling." Oklahoman (January 26, 1986):97.
"A Reception thank you." Oklahoman (February 11, 1987):50.
Kathryn Jensen White. "Annual storytelling fest not just for young people." Oklahoman (January 29, 1988):88.
Linda Lynn. "Storytelling art reflects cultures."

Oklahoman (January 27, 1989): 76.

"Reception honors festival participants." Oklahoman (February 1, 1989):25.

"Council schedules storytelling festival." Oklahoman (January 18, 1991):46.

"Storytellers to share yarns at 10th Wintertales festival." Oklahoman (January 2, 1991):68.

Sandi Davis. "Storytellers swarm to city." Oklahoman (February 16, 1992):85.

"Storytelling festival readied." Oklahoman (February 4, 1998):51.

"Top storytellers to offer tales." Oklahoman (Feb. 15, 1998):93.

Sandy Davis. "Festival highlights storytelling festival." Oklahoman (February 16, 1999): 41.

Marcia Shottenkirk. "Local celebrities among storytellers." Oklahoman (February 4, 1999):10.

"21st Annual Wintertales storytelling festival." Brochure. Indicates four people from Territory Tellers conducted workshops: Connie Fisher, Marilyn A. Hudson, and Roger Harris. Featured tellers were Patrick Ball, Gladys Gogswell, Angela Lloyd, and Ed Stivender. Author collection.

"23 Annual Winter Tales." Territory Tattler (Winter 2003-04):1.

"Oklahoma Olio." Flyer; Wintertales. Territory Tellers , 2004.

"Wintertales." Territory Tattler (Winter 2007):2.

"Wintertales." Territory Tattler (Winter 2008):3.

# ABOUT THE AUTHOR

Marilyn A. Hudson is an author and researcher who loves turning over history to see the story long hidden by time. A graduate of the University of Oklahoma with degrees in history and in library and information studies, she collects arcane tales and has been dubbed the "genie of bizarre history."

Hudson is author of several historical monographs, such as, *When Death Rode the Rails, Tales of Hell's Half Acre, Halloween: Oklahoma Tricks and Treats, Murderous Marriages, The Windows of Wesley,* several organizational histories and a biography, *Noel Brooks: A Life Shining and Burning.*

She also writes fiction such as the short story collection *The Bones of Summe*r, the Madame Delaine series and is co-author of the novel. *The Mound.* Her novel, *Foul Harvest,* is due out fall of 2014.

She lives with her husband in Norman, Oklahoma surrounded by a crowd of imaginary playmates who help her create stories – but don't tell anyone!

To contact her directly:

marilyahudson@yahoo.coom

# STORYTELLING ORGANIZATIONS

## National

National Storytelling Network http://www.storynet.org/

The National Storytelling Network is dedicated to advancing the art of storytelling – as a performing art, a process of cultural transformation, and more.

Network of Biblical Storytellers
http://www.nbsint.org/

This organization is dedicated to the use of storytelling as a viable communication tool in sharing the Bible. Stories used are drawn from and reflect the Biblical text.

## State

Territory Tellers
www.territorytellers.org

This non-profit 501.C3 storytelling organization offers memberships at the individual and corporate supporting levels. They sponsor an annual storytelling festival and encourage storytelling across the state through various storytelling groups or guilds.

5658 NW Pioneer Circle

Norman, Oklahoma 73072

www.whorlbooks.blogspot.com

YOUR CLUE TO GREAT READS

whorlbooks@gmail.com

marilynahudson@gmail.com

"STORIES  CENTER STAGE!"